SOCIO-ECONOMIC SURVEYS
of Two Villages in Rajasthan

A STUDY OF AGRARIAN RELATIONS

SOCIO-ECONOMIC SURVEYS
of Two Villages in Rajasthan

A STUDY OF AGRARIAN RELATIONS

Edited by

Madhura Swaminathan and Vikas Rawal

Research and Writing

Vikas Rawal   Madhura Swaminathan
Arindam Das   Pallavi Chavan
Aparajita Bakshi   Venkatesh Athreya
Niladri Sekhar Dhar   Shamsher Singh
Jayan Jose Thomas   Biplab Sarkar
Yasodhara Das   A. Bheemeshwar Reddy

Foundation for
Agrarian
Studies

Tulika Books

Published by

Tulika Books

35 A/1, Shahpur Jat, New Delhi 110 049

in association with

Foundation for Agrarian Studies

www.agrarianstudies.org

© Foundation for Agrarian Studies 2015

First published in India 2015

ISBN: 978-93-82381-67-9

Printed at Chaman Enterprises, Delhi 110 002

Preface

In 2005, the Foundation for Agrarian Studies (FAS) initiated its Project on Agrarian Relations in India (PARI), with the aim of studying, *inter alia*, village-level production, production systems, livelihoods, and the socio-economic characteristics of different strata of the rural population, by means of detailed village surveys. The Project on Agrarian Relations in India, that was initiated by and is currently supervised by V.K. Ramachandran, has so far covered twenty-two villages in ten States of India.

In the Rajasthan round of 2007, two villages were surveyed: Dungariya, a tribal village in Udaipur district, and 25 F Gulabewala from the Gang Canal region of Sri Ganganagar district. A third village, Rewasi in Sikar district, which could not be studied in 2007, was surveyed in 2010. Each of the villages is located in a different agro-ecological region of Rajasthan: Dungariya is in the Sub-Humid Southern Plain and Aravali Hills region, 25F Gulabewala is in the Irrigated North Western Plain region, and Rewasi is in the Transitional Plain of Inland Drainage region. The choice of villages was made in consultation with the Rajasthan Committee of the All India Kisan Sabha.

The village of 25 F Gulabewala is irrigated by the Gang Canal project. The main crops cultivated in Gulabewala at the time of the survey were wheat, rapeseed, cotton, cluster beans, and fodder crops. The village was character-ised by large landholdings and mechanised agriculture. Rewasi is a semi-arid village characterised by sandy soils and low rainfall, where pearl millet is the most important crop of the kharif season. The year of the survey, 2009–10, was one of low rainfall in Rewasi and the kharif crops were almost completely destroyed. Animal resources – the people tend cattle, camels, and goats – were an important source of household income in this village. Another important aspect of the village economy was migration, particularly by men, to other cities in India and abroad. The third village, Dungariya, is a small, forest-fringe, tribal village. Since a detailed report on the economy of this village has been published in Ramachandran (2010), a report on Dungariya is not included in this book.

A census survey was conducted in the three selected villages. A unique feature of the survey is the estimation of household incomes, based on detailed information on income from crop production, animal resources, agricultural and non-agricultural wage labour, salaries, business and trade, rent, interest earnings, pensions, remittances, scholarships, and other sources.

The structure of this book is as follows. Chapter 1 provides a brief introduction to the rural economy of Rajasthan with a focus on the three districts to which the study villages belong. Chapters 2 and 3 discuss the socio-economic features of 25 F Gulabewala and Rewasi villages respectively. Some comparative findings from the three villages are pulled together in Chapter 4.

The book draws heavily on presentations made at the "Meeting on the Results from Village Surveys, Rajasthan Round", held in Jaipur from 3 to 5 March 2012, and the comments and discussions that followed. We are grateful to Amra Ram, Subhashini Ali, Duli Chand, Vasudev, Rajiv Gupta, Rajni Palriwala, V. Sridhar and other participants at the Jaipur meeting for their active support and critical questioning. The presentations made at the meeting and the authors of these presentations are listed at the end of this book.

Further contributions during the writing of this book came from Venkatesh Athreya, Aparajita Bakshi, Pallavi Chavan, Arindam Das, Yasodhara Das, Niladri Sekhar Dhar, Bheemeshwar Reddy, Jayan Jose Thomas, Vikas Rawal, Biplab Sarkar, Shamsher Singh, and Madhura Swaminathan. Aditi Dixit and Shamsher Singh helped with final revisions of the manuscript. Research assistance at different stages was provided by Nabanita Adhikari, Amalendu Das, Sumit Bhaduri, Koustav Dutta, Pinki Ghosh, Navpreet Kaur, and T. Sivamurugan.

A research grant from the University Grants Commission provided support to Vikas Rawal. Madhura Swaminathan is grateful to the Indian Statistical Institute, Bangalore Centre, for providing an excellent environment for research and writing.

MADHURA SWAMINATHAN   VIKAS RAWAL
Bengaluru   *New Delhi*

31 August 2015

Contents

Tables, Maps, Figures

CHAPTER 1

Chapter 2

CHAPTER 3

1

Features of the Rural Economy
of Rajasthan, with special reference to
Sri Ganganagar, Sikar and Udaipur Districts

The three villages of Rajasthan that formed part of the PARI (Project on Agrarian Relations in India) village study programme belong to three different districts and three different agro-climatic regions of the State. We provide, here, a brief overview of agriculture and other features of the rural economy in Rajasthan, with special reference to the three districts of Sri Ganganagar, Sikar and Udaipur.[1]

AGRICULTURE AND LIVESTOCK

According to the Census of 2011, 75 per cent of Rajasthan's population lived in rural areas. Cultivators and agricultural workers accounted for 62 per cent of the State's work force. However, while a large proportion of the population was dependent on agriculture, agriculture and allied activities accounted for only 30 per cent of the gross state domestic product in the year 2010–11.

Animal resources constitute an extremely important component of the rural economy of Rajasthan. In 2008–09, the latest year for which disaggregated data are available, animal resources contributed about 11 per cent of the gross state domestic product. To put this in perspective, animal resources accounted for only 3.2 per cent of national gross domestic product in the same year.

---

[1] Statistics used in this section have been taken from different volumes of *Agricultural Statistics, Rajasthan*, published by the Directorate of Economics and Statistics, Government of Rajasthan.

Map 1.1 *Location of study villages in map of India*

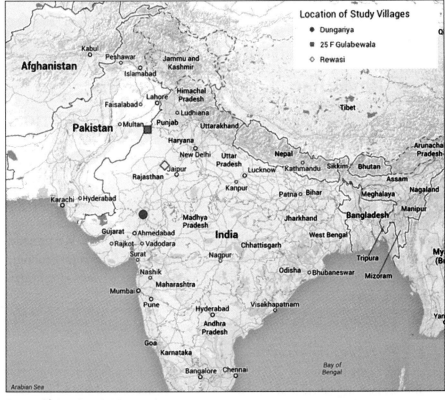

Prepared using Google Maps engine.

LAND USE

As per the land use statistics for 2010–11, only 53 per cent of the reported area in Rajasthan was cultivated. Different types of fallow land, culturable waste land, permanent pastures and barren land accounted for another 33 per cent of the reported area. Eight per cent of the land was under forests, and about 5 per cent was put to non-agricultural uses.

There were, of course, stark differences across districts. In Udaipur, forests accounted for 28.6 per cent of the area, and another 22.7 per cent of the reported area was classified as barren and uncultivable land. In 2010–11, the net sown area was only about 17 per cent of the reported area. In contrast, net sown area accounted for about 70 per cent of the reported area in Sikar and Sri Ganganagar districts (Table 1.1).

Map 1.2 *Location of study villages in map of Rajasthan*

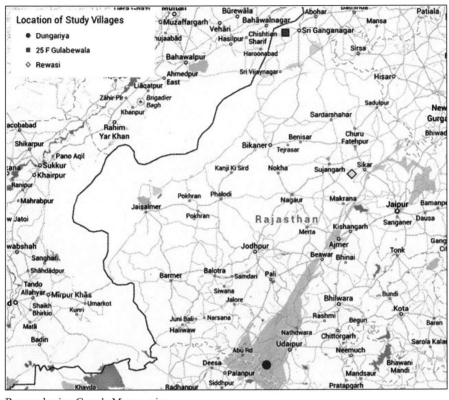

Prepared using Google Maps engine.

IRRIGATION

Agriculture in Rajasthan is primarily rainfed. In 2010–11, only 36 per cent of the total net sown area of the State was irrigated (Table 1.2). Of the net irrigated area, 73 per cent was irrigated by groundwater and 25 per cent was irrigated by canals.

Of the three districts, the extent of availability of irrigation is lowest in Udaipur. Only 32 per cent of net sown area of Udaipur was irrigated in 2010–11. Open wells were the main source of irrigation here. In Sikar district, about 45 per cent of net sown area was irrigated, of which about two-thirds were irrigated by tubewells and the rest by open wells.

By contrast, Sri Ganganagar may be characterised as a canal-irrigated district. About 75 per cent of the net sown area in this district was irrigated in 2010–11, and over 99 per cent of the irrigated area was fed by irrigation canals. Irrigation in Sri Ganganagar district comes from the Gang canal and the Bhakhra canal, both part of the Indira Gandhi Nahar Pariyojana (IGNP) irrigation scheme. The Gang canal has a larger command area: about 50 per cent of the net irrigated area of the district.

Table 1.1 *Area of land under different uses as percentage of total reported area, study districts and Rajasthan, 2010–11* (per cent)

Land use	Sri Ganganagar	Sikar	Udaipur	Rajasthan
Forest	5.5	7.9	28.6	8.0
Current fallow	5.4	4.3	1.2	3.6
Fallow land other than current fallow	7.7	5.3	4.2	5.0
Culturable waste land	3.7	1.1	8.6	12.4
Permanent pastures and other grazing land	0.0	5.2	6.0	4.9
Land under miscellaneous tree crops and groves	0.7	0.0	0.0	0.1
Barren and unculturable land	0.2	2.4	22.7	6.9
Area under non-agricultural use	6.4	4.6	11.2	5.5
Net sown area	70.4	69.2	17.4	53.5
Reported area	100.0	100.0	100.0	100.0

Source: Agricultural Statistics of Rajasthan, 2010–11.

Table 1.2 *Share of different sources in net irrigated area, study districts and Rajasthan, 2010–11* (per cent)

Source	Sri Ganganagar	Sikar	Udaipur	Rajasthan
Canals	99.2	0.0	2.8	24.5
Tubewells	0.7	67.2	12.6	41.9
Open wells	0.1	32.8	76.4	31.7
Other sources	0.0	0.0	7.9	1.9
Total	100.0	100.0	100.0	100.0
Net irrigated area as a proportion of net sown area	74.7	45.1	31.8	36.3

Source: Agricultural Statistics of Rajasthan, 2010–11.

Map 1.3 *Agro-climatic regions of Rajasthan*

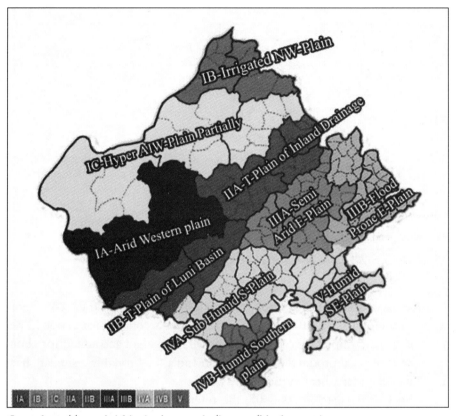

Source: http://www.krishi.rajasthan.gov.in/images/blank_copy.jpg

CROPPING PATTERN

Given the low levels of irrigation, cultivators in Rajasthan have specialised in cultivating crops that are less water-intensive, namely, oilseeds, millets and pulses. Rajasthan is the second largest producer of oilseeds in the country after Madhya Pradesh; it accounts for about 20 per cent of the national production of oilseeds. It is the largest producer of rapeseed and mustard; in 2010–11, Rajasthan's share in national production of rapeseed and mustard was about 53 per cent. In the same year, Rajasthan accounted for about 16 per cent of the production of millets; it was the largest producer of pearl millet, accounting for about 44 per cent of national production.

Table 1.3 *Area under selected crops as share of gross cropped area (GCA), study districts, different years* (per cent)

Crop	Sri Ganganagar 2006–07	Sikar 2009–10	Udaipur 2006–07
Bajra (Pearl millet)	1.5	42.5	–
Cotton	15.1	–	–
Cluster bean seed	13.0	9.4	3.7
Maize	–	–	46.7
Wheat	20.8	12.7	22.0
Rapeseed and Mustard	30.0	8.3	5.1
Gram	8.2	4.4	3.9
Gross cropped area	100.0	100.0	100.0
Gross cropped area (in hectares)	926832	715042	403849

Source: Agricultural Statistics of Rajasthan, 2006–07 and 2009–10.

In terms of share of gross cropped area (GCA), wheat was the second most important crop of Rajasthan. In 2010–11, wheat accounted for about 12 per cent of gross cropped area. In the same year, Rajasthan accounted for about 8 per cent of total production of wheat in India (and roughly a similar share in total area under wheat in the country).

In Sri Ganganagar, in 2006–07, the reference year of the survey, cotton (15 per cent of GCA) and cluster bean (13 per cent of GCA) were the major kharif crops. Rapeseed and mustard (30 per cent of GCA), wheat (21 per cent of GCA) and gram (8 per cent of GCA) were the major rabi crops. In Sikar, in 2009–10, the reference year of the survey, pearl millet (42.5 per cent of GCA) and cluster bean (9.4 per cent of GCA) were the major kharif crops. Wheat (12.7 per cent of GCA), and rapeseed and mustard (8.3 per cent of GCA) were the major rabi crops. In Udaipur, on the other hand, in 2006–07, maize (47 per cent of GCA) was the major kharif crop and wheat (22 per cent of GCA) was the major rabi crop. (See Table 1.3.)

ADOPTION OF MODERN BIOCHEMICAL INPUTS

Table 1.4 shows that the extent of adoption of high-yielding varieties of seeds was high in the case of wheat but lagged behind substantially in other cereal

Table 1.4 *Proportion of area sown with high-yielding varieties of seeds, selected crops, study districts and Rajasthan, different years* (per cent)

Level	Crop		
	Wheat	Pearl millet	Maize
Sri Ganganagar	100.0	–	–
Sikar	85.5	73.9	–
Udaipur	68.8	–	51.6
Rajasthan	93.3	45.0	72.4

Source: Agricultural Statistics of Rajasthan, 2006–07 and 2009–10.

crops. In 2010–11, high-yielding varieties were grown on about 93 per cent of the land sown with wheat, but only 45 per cent of land sown with pearl millet had high-yielding varieties. Of the three study districts, the extent of adoption of high-yielding varieties of seeds was highest in Sri Ganganagar (100 per cent for wheat), followed by Sikar (85 per cent for wheat and 74 per cent for pearl millet), and lowest in Udaipur (69 per cent for wheat and 51 per cent for maize).

The use of chemical fertilizers per hectare of cropped area was low in Rajasthan. In 2010–11, on average, the extent of use of chemical fertilizers was about 43 kilograms per hectare; the corresponding figure for India as a whole was 112 kilograms per hectare.

COSTS AND RETURNS FROM CULTIVATION

An analysis of unit-level data from the Comprehensive Scheme for studying the Cost of Cultivation of Principal Crops in India (CCPC) shows large variations in the returns from crop cultivation across regions, crops and cultivators (see Appendix 1). Of the main crops grown in the three regions to which the study villages belong, cotton, which was cultivated in the kharif season in the Irrigated North-Western (INW) Plain region, was the most profitable. As per the CCPC data, average returns (gross value of output minus cost A2) from the cultivation of cotton in the INW region were Rs 34,210 per acre. In contrast, returns from the main kharif crops cultivated in the Transitional Plain of Inland Drainage (TPID) region (Rs 5,487 per acre for bajra) and in the Sub-humid Southern Plains/Hills (SSPH) region (Rs 2,012 per acre for maize) were very low. Data on returns for wheat, which was the most important rabi crop in all the three regions, also show that the returns (over Cost A2) were highest in the INW region (Rs 20,969 per acre), followed by the TPID region (Rs 14,343 per acre), and lowest in the SSPH region (Rs 7,894 per acre). (See Table A1.1.)

ACCESS TO FORMAL-SECTOR CREDIT

Rajasthan is a relatively under-banked State of the country, although a part of the well-banked northern region of India. The strength of bank branch network and disbursement of bank credit in Rajasthan, particularly in its rural areas, is well below the all-India and northern region average. To illustrate, in 2010, there was a branch for every 18,128 persons in rural Rajasthan while there was one branch for every 15,755 persons in rural India. A more detailed analysis of changes in rural credit in Rajasthan is presented in Appendix 2.

There was considerable variation in the extent of banking development across districts. Sri Ganganagar district was a well-banked district in the State. It was above the State average in terms of the two indicators of banking development considered here: population per bank branch and bank credit per capita (Table 1.5). The ratio of bank credit to gross district domestic product in Sri Ganganagar was 27 per cent in 2010. The rural areas in the district were also well-banked showing a lower rural population per bank branch and higher rural credit per capita than the State average (Table 1.6). Sikar was a relatively backward district in terms of banking development. Rural areas of Udaipur district were the worst off among these three districts in terms of population per bank branch and credit per capita.

Table 1.5 *Select banking indicators, study districts and Rajasthan, 2010*

State/district	Population per bank branch (000s)	Total credit per capita (Rs)	Total credit as per cent of district domestic product	Remark (based on population per bank branch)
Sri Ganganagar	11.3	14000	27	Above State average
Sikar	18.6	5900	18	Below State average
Udaipur	14.4	12300	31	Above State average
Rajasthan	15.9	14000	35	–

Source: Reserve Bank of India, *Basic Statistical Returns of Scheduled Commercial Banks in India*, various issues; www.statistics.rajasthan.gov.in; censusindia.gov.in

Table 1.6 *Select rural banking indicators, study districts and Rajasthan, 2010*

State/district	Rural population per branch (000s)	Rural credit per capita (Rs)	Remark (based on population per bank branch)
Sri Ganganagar	12.5	12100	Above State average
Sikar	18.4	5700	Below State average
Udaipur	23.8	3000	Below State average
Rajasthan	17.8	5500	–

Source: Reserve Bank of India, *Basic Statistical Returns of Scheduled Commercial Banks in India*, various issues; censusindia.gov.in

Table 1.7 *Rural population per bank branch, study districts and Rajasthan, different years* (000 persons)

Year	Sri Ganganagar	Sikar	Udaipur	Rajasthan
1995	13.6	18.6	18.8	15.0
2000	13.1	18.9	21.7	16.8
2005	13.5	19.2	22.9	18.2
2006	13.7	19.5	23.0	18.1
2011	12.2	16.0	23.0	16.6

Note: See note to Appendix 2, Table A2.2.
Source: Reserve Bank of India, *Basic Statistical Returns of Scheduled Commercial Banks in India*, various issues; censusindia.gov.in

After 2006, there was an expansion in the branch network in rural areas of Rajasthan. This was also seen in the rural areas of Sikar and Sri Ganganagar districts; the increase was particularly impressive in Sikar district (Table 1.7). The rural population per bank branch fell from 19,500 in 2006 to 16,000 in 2011 in Sikar. In Udaipur, however, there was little change in the bank branch network.

SELECTED ASPECTS OF HUMAN DEVELOPMENT IN RAJASTHAN

Rajasthan, part of the BIMARU group of States (comprising Bihar, Madhya Pradesh, Rajasthan and Uttar Pradesh), is known for a poor record in respect of development in the areas of education and health, and for high levels of gender and caste disparities. While a comprehensive assessment of the developmental gaps in Rajasthan is beyond the scope of this chapter, it would be useful to provide a few summary statistics to contextualise the study.

As per the 2011 Census, only 45.8 per cent of rural women and 76 per cent of rural men in Rajasthan were literate (Table 1.8). In 2001, Rajasthan had the lowest literacy rate for rural women among all the States of India. There was a substantial gap in respect of ensuring universal schooling among rural children in Rajasthan. As per the 66th Round of the National Sample Survey (NSS), in Rajasthan, 84 per cent of rural children in the age-group 6–14 years attended school; the corresponding figure for India was 88 per cent. Among rural girls aged 6–14 years in Rajasthan, only 79 per cent attended school; the corresponding proportion for India was 86 per cent (Rawal 2011).

Rajasthan's record in respect of gender disparities is particularly poor. As

Table 1.8 *Number of literates as proportion of population (aged 7 years and above), rural population, study districts, Rajasthan and India, 2011* (per cent)

District/State	Female	Male	Person	Gender gap in literacy rate
Sri Ganganagar	55.3	75.9	66.2	20.6
Sikar	56.4	84.9	70.8	28.5
Udaipur	39.8	69.6	54.9	29.8
Rajasthan	45.8	76.2	61.4	30.4
India	57.9	77.2	67.8	19.3

Source: Census of India, 2011.

Table 1.9 *Sex ratio and child (0–6 years old) sex ratio of rural population, study districts, Rajasthan and India, 2011* (women per 1000 men)

District/State	Sex ratio	Child sex ratio
Sri Ganganagar	891	859
Sikar	951	843
Udaipur	966	933
Rajasthan	933	892
India	949	923

Source: Census of India, 2011.

per the 2011 Census, the rural sex ratio was only 933 women per 1,000 men (Table 1.9). Among rural children aged 6 years or less, the sex ratio was 892 girls per 1,000 boys. Of the three study districts, Sri Ganganagar had the lowest (891 women per 1,000 men) sex ratio. Child sex ratios were 843 girls per 1,000 boys in Sikar and 859 girls per 1,000 boys in Sri Ganganagar. Udaipur district's better-than-average performance in terms of sex ratio can be explained by the high proportion of Scheduled Tribes (STs) in the population of the district: Scheduled Tribes constituted 50 per cent of the total population and 60 per cent of the rural population in 2011.

The access of rural households in Rajasthan to basic amenities like toilets and drinking water was also very poor (Table 1.10). As per the 2011 census, less than 20 per cent of rural households in Rajasthan had any kind of latrine facility within the premises of their house. Similarly, only 21 per cent of rural households had a source of drinking water within premises of their house. Sikar was clearly worse off than Sri Ganganagar in respect of all basic amenities. Among the selected districts, Udaipur stands out as the most under-developed in respect of these basic amenities. In Udaipur, only 9 per cent of rural households had latrines and only 12 per cent of rural households had drinking water facilities within the premises of their house.

On another indicator of housing, the proportion of households living in pucca or permanent structures, Ganganagar was the worst performing district: only 28 per cent households lived in houses where the roof and walls were made of permanent materials.

It is of note that while Sri Ganganagar district tops the three districts in

Table 1.10 *Proportion of rural households having* pucca *houses, latrine and drinking water facilities within premises of house, study districts, Rajasthan and India, 2011* (per cent)

District/State	Latrine	Drinking water	*Pucca**/permanent house
Sri Ganganagar	81.3	55.1	28
Sikar	40.2	38.5	86
Udaipur	9.3	12.0	38
Rajasthan	19.6	21.0	57
India	30.7	35.0	44

Note: * A *pucca* house is one which has both roof and walls made of *pucca* materials such as burnt brick/tile, cement, iron, concrete, stone, asbestos and metal sheet.
Source: Census of India, 2011.

Table 1.11 *Human Development Index (HDI) and its component indices, study districts, 2007*

District	Education HDI	Health HDI	Income HDI	Overall HDI
Sri Ganganagar	0.787	0.816	0.825	0.809
Sikar	0.837	0.830	0.428	0.698
Udaipur	0.761	0.413	0.611	0.595

Source: Rajasthan Human Development Report: An Update, 2008.

terms of overall levels of agricultural and economic development, it has lower literacy rates than Sikar, and the lowest sex ratio of all three districts. A summary measure of capability enhancement is the Human Development Index (HDI), which is based on attainments in education, health and standard of living or incomes. The HDI estimated for the districts of Rajasthan shows that Sri Ganganagar district had the highest HDI in the State. The HDI for Sri Ganganagar was 0.809 whereas that for Sikar district was 0.698 and Udaipur district was even lower, with an HDI of 0.595. While Sri Ganganagar tops the three districts in terms of income index, it ranks lower than Sikar in both education and health indices (Table 1.11).

APPENDIX 1
COST OF CULTIVATION AND RETURNS FROM CULTIVATION IN RAJASTHAN: AN ANALYSIS OF CCPC DATA

Vikas Rawal

Official statistics on cost of cultivation and returns from farming are collected under the Comprehensive Scheme for Studying the Cost of Cultivation of Principal Crops (CCPC) of the Directorate of Economics and Statistics, Ministry of Agriculture, Government of India. In this note, I analyse CCPC unit data for Rajasthan, disaggregated at the sub-regional level.

Before presenting an analysis of the data from CCPC surveys, it is important to mention a major limitation of these statistics, namely: although the data are collected for all crops cultivated by sample cultivators, at the stage of processing, the data are separated crop-wise and are validated only for selected crops. These are then released separately for each of the crops. The data for all inter-crops and mixed crops are also separated at the stage of preliminary data processing. This is a serious limitation since most peasants grow multiple crops on their operational holdings within a season, as well as grow crops in more than one season in a given agricultural year.

Until recently, reports of the Commission for Agricultural Costs and Prices (CACP) were the main source of CCPC data. These reports provided only State-wise averages of per hectare output and per hectare expenditure. The Directorate of Economics and Statistics has recently made available farm-by-farm CCPC data, separately for individual crops. Availability of farm-by-farm data allows us to analyse the distribution of costs and returns at the level of agro-ecological regions within the State. However, because of the separation of data between individual crops, such analysis cannot be done at the level of farm households or jointly for inter-crops.

The CCPC surveys also suffer from several limitations. The survey schedule is outdated and does not adequately capture many changes in systems of agricultural production that have taken place in recent times. Comparison of CCPC data with statistics on cost of cultivation collected as part of the Project on Agrarian Relations in India (PARI) suggests that the CCPC surveys tend to underestimate costs and overestimate returns. There are many reasons for this including an underestimation of tenancy and rental costs (in estimates of paid-out cost). Also, all observations where the crop has entirely failed and the output is zero are systematically removed from CCPC data at the stage of processing. This too results in overestimation of average returns and underestimation of the proportion of cultivators having negative or lower-than-average returns. This problem is likely to be particularly serious in an arid State like Rajasthan where crop failures are not uncommon.

Figures A1.1 to A1.6 show trends in gross value of output (GVO), cost A2 and net returns (GVO – cost A2) for different crops between 1994–95 and 2010–11.[2] The upper panel of each figure shows the trend of average net returns between 1995–96 and 2010–11. Box-plots in the top panel show the distribution of net returns across individual farms in each year during this period. The lower panel of each figure shows the average gross value of output (GVO) divided between cost A2 and net returns. Each figure shows trends for Rajasthan as a whole, and for the three regions where the three study villages are located: Irrigated North Western (INW) Plain region (where 25 F Gulabewala is located), Transitional Plain of Inland Drainage (TPID) region (where Rewasi is located), and Sub-humid Southern Plain and Aravali Hills (SSPH) region (where Dungariya is located).

To convert values to real prices, the gross output, costs and net returns were converted into equivalent quantities of the main product (grain or fibre) using farm-gate prices reported for each producer. These were then converted into constant 2010–11 rupee values using average grain price in 2010–11 for that crop. It may be noted that the conversion to real prices is done for each crop using output prices for that crop. Since relative prices of different crops change over time (since price trends across crops are varied), comparison of levels and trends across crops should be made with care.

First, the figures show that, in any year, there are wide variations in levels of net returns obtained by different cultivators across and within different regions. Policies on price support in India typically take into account the average returns obtained by cultivators in a State without accounting for the wide variation across different regions of a State and across cultivators within each region. The figures show that, despite a distortion in the distribution because of removal of all cases of crop failure, for each crop, a large proportion of the cultivators got less-than-average returns.

Secondly, of the main crops cultivated in the study villages, cotton, cultivated

---

[2] Cost A2 refers broadly to all paid-out costs (as defined by CCPC).

Figure A1.1 *Gross value of output, cost A2 and net returns from cultivation of bajra, Rajasthan* (Rs per acre) (2010–11 bajra prices)

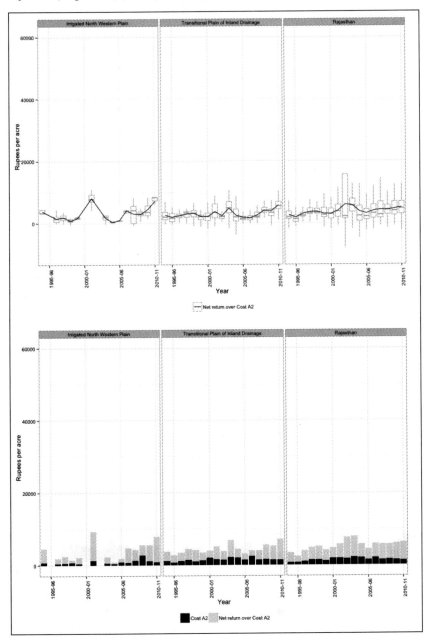

Source: Author's estimates based on CCPC data.

Figure A1.2 *Gross value of output, cost A2 and net returns from cultivation of maize, Rajasthan* (Rs per acre) (2010–11 maize prices)

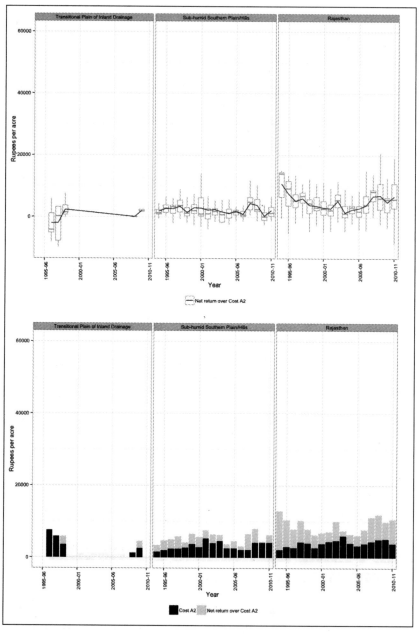

Source: Author's estimates based on CCPC data.

Figure A1.3 *Gross value of output, cost A2 and net returns from cultivation of cotton, Rajasthan* (Rs per acre) (2010–11 cotton prices)

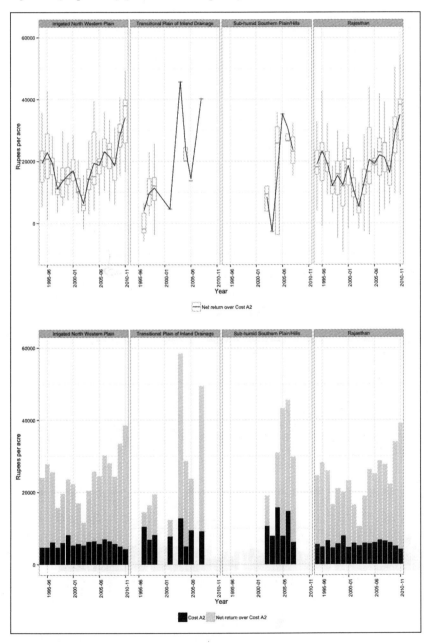

Source: Author's estimates based on CCPC data.

Figure A1.4 *Gross value of output, cost A2 and net returns from cultivation of wheat, Rajasthan* (Rs per acre) (2010–11 wheat prices)

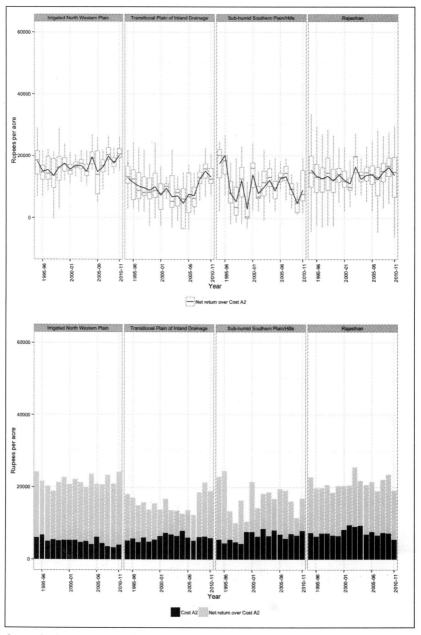

Source: Author's estimates based on CCPC data.

Figure A1.5 *Gross value of output, cost A2 and net returns from cultivation of mustard and rapeseed, Rajasthan* (Rs per acre) (2010–11 prices of mustard and rapeseed)

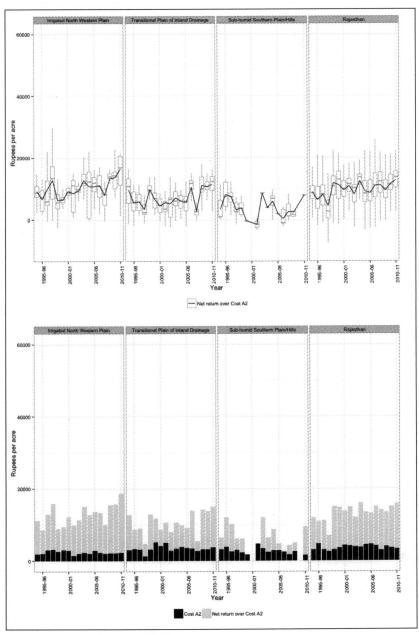

Source: Author's estimates based on CCPC data.

Figure A1.6 *Gross value of output, cost A2 and net returns from cultivation of gram, Rajasthan* (Rs per acre) (2010–11 gram prices)

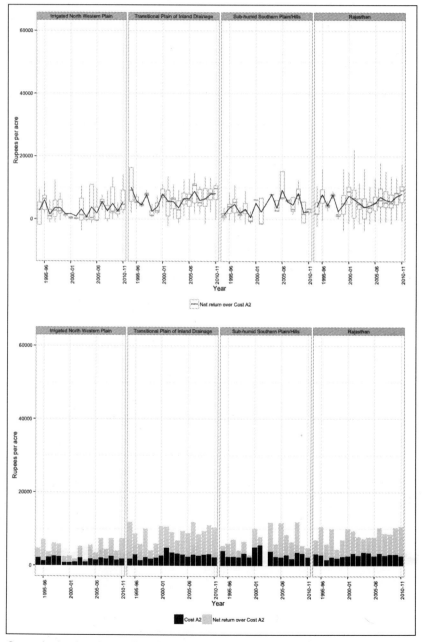

Source: Author's estimates based on CCPC data.

in the kharif season in the INW Plain region, has the highest returns. Since this is the main cotton-growing region in Rajasthan, the levels and trends for the State closely resemble the levels and trends seen here. Average returns from cultivation of cotton in the INW Plain region, in terms of 2010–11 cotton prices, declined from about Rs 20,000 per acre in the mid-1990s to about Rs 6,300 per acre in 2002–03. With the increase in global prices of cotton since then, there has been a sharp rise in average returns from cotton cultivation over the years, reaching Rs 34,210 per acre in 2010–11. In contrast, bajra, the most important kharif crop in the TPID region, and maize, the most important kharif crop of the SSPH region, gave very low levels of returns (Table A1.1). Among the rabi crops, average returns were highest in wheat cultivation, followed by rapeseed and mustard, and lowest for gram.

Thirdly, the average levels and trends of output, costs and returns in different regions varied from the State averages (which are averages over nine different regions of Rajasthan). For all the crops, average returns in the SSPH region were considerably lower than the State average.

Of the three regions in which the study villages are located, regional variation was particularly notable for the major rabi crops as these were cultivated in all three regions. For example, in the case of wheat, average levels of returns in the TPID region and SSPH region were considerably lower than in the INW region and in Rajasthan as a whole. Between 1994–95 and 2010–11, the average levels of returns in the INW region fluctuated between Rs 15,000 to Rs 21,000 per acre (at constant 2010–11 wheat prices). Over the same period,

Table A1.1 *Average net return over cost A2, by crop and region, Rajasthan, 2010* (Rs per acre)

Crop	Irrigated North Western (INW) Plain	Transitional Plain of Inland Drainage (TPID)	Sub-humid Southern Plain/Hills (SSPH)	Rajasthan
Bajra (Pearl millet)	6916	5487	–	4998
Maize	–	–	2012	7158
Cotton	34210	–	–	34883
Wheat	20969	14343	7894	13806
Mustard and Rapeseed	17541	10482	8175	12724
Gram	5577	8181	2434	8045

Source: Author's estimates based on CCPC data.

in Rajasthan as a whole, returns from wheat fluctuated between Rs 11,000 to Rs 16,000 per acre (at constant 2010–11 wheat prices). In contrast, in the TPID region, average returns from wheat cultivation declined between 1994–95 and 2004–05. In 1994–95, the average return from wheat cultivation was Rs 12,800 per acre; this declined to Rs 4,720 per acre in 2004–05. There was a recovery in the levels of returns after 2004–05, with the average return rising to Rs 14,343 per acre in 2010–11. In the INW region, there was a rise in returns from cultivation of rapeseed and mustard between the mid-1990s and the end of the 2000s, and a closing of the gap between returns obtained from wheat cultivation and returns obtained from cultivation of rapeseed and mustard.

In 2010–11, the average return from cultivation of rapeseed and mustard in the region was Rs 17,541 per acre. In the other two regions, no clear trend was observed in the average returns from rapeseed and mustard. In the TPID region, the average returns fluctuated between Rs 4,000 and Rs 11,000 per acre. In the SSPH region, average returns from cultivation of rapeseed and mustard fluctuated between a loss of Rs 1,500 per acre and a positive return of about Rs 8,000 per acre. In case of gram, among the three regions, highest output and returns were obtained in the TPID region. In 2010–11, average return from cultivation of gram was Rs 8,181 per acre in the TPID region, Rs 5,577 per acre in the INW region, and Rs 2,434 per acre in the SSPH region.

APPENDIX 2
RAJASTHAN: AN UNDERBANKED STATE

Pallavi Chavan

Rajasthan is a relatively underbanked State in the country. It belongs to the relatively well-banked northern region of India but is positioned low within the region. In 2011, there were 14,900 persons per bank branch in Rajasthan as against the regional average of 9,800 persons and national average of 13,100 persons (Table A2.1). Similarly, the extent of bank credit per capita in 2011 was Rs 16,900 in Rajasthan, much lower than the corresponding regional and national averages of Rs 60,100 and Rs 33,700 respectively.

The extent of development of banking in rural areas of Rajasthan was even less satisfactory. In 2011, there were 17,000 persons per bank branch in rural Rajasthan. For rural India as a whole, the population per bank branch was 15,200 persons in the same year (Table A2.2).

It is now well established that banking services in rural areas were adversely affected by the policies of financial liberalisation begun in 1991 (Shetty 2005; Ramachandran and Swaminathan 2005; Chavan 2005). There was a decline in the network of rural branches across India including in Rajasthan. The population per bank branch in Rajasthan rose from 15,000 persons in 1995 to 17,800 persons in 2005. After 2006, however, there was a slight improvement in the

Table A2.1 *Indicators of banking development, by region, India and Rajasthan, 2011*

Region	Population per branch	Amount of credit per capita (Rs)
Western	12100	79400
Northern	9800	60100
Rajasthan	14900	16900
Southern	9800	43400
Eastern	17900	11700
Central	16900	9300
North-eastern	18900	7000
All-India	13100	33700

Source: Authors' calculations based on *Basic Statistical Returns of Scheduled Commercial Banks in India*, various issues; GoI (1991; 2001); censusindia.gov.in.

Table A2.2 *Number of rural persons per bank branch, Rajasthan and India, 1995–2011* (000s)

State	Classification based on Census of 1991			Classification based on Census of 2001	
	1995	2002	2005	2006	2011
Rajasthan	15.0	16.5	17.8	18.5	17.0
India	14.6	15.2	16.6	17.3	15.2

Notes: 1. There is a problem in comparing Reserve Bank of India (RBI) data on bank branches by population groups across years. This is because the classification of bank centres and branches servicing these centres changes as and when data from the new Population Census are used by the RBI. The RBI followed the Census of 1991 between 1995 and 2005, and the Census of 2001 from 2006 onwards.
2. The RBI provides branch data on 'rural centres' (having a population of less than 10,000 persons) and 'semi-urban centres' (having a population ranging 10,000 and above but less than 0.1 million persons). We have aggregated 'rural' and 'semi-urban' branches and considered this total as rural area branches in the Table.
Source: Author's calculations based on *Basic Statistical Returns of Scheduled Commercial Banks in India*, various issues; GoI (1991; 2001); censusindia.gov.in.

rural branch network, resulting in a fall in the population per bank branch from 18,500 persons in 2006 to 17,000 persons in 2011.[3] This increase can be attributed to the new emphasis on financial inclusion and improving the presence of banks in rural areas after 2005 (Ramakumar and Chavan 2011; Chavan 2013).

The share of formal sources in total debt of rural households in Rajasthan has been generally much lower than the national average; this supports the point made earlier about Rajasthan being an underbanked State (Table A2.3). In 2002, about 34 per cent of the total debt of rural households was from formal sources, when the national average was 57 per cent.

Between 1991 and 2002 – the decade of initiation of financial liberalisation – there was a fall in the share of formal sources in total debt of rural households across almost all States of India including Rajasthan (Table A2.3). The main decline was on account of commercial banks. The share of commercial banks in total debt came down from 25.4 per cent in 1991 to 21 per cent in 2002 (NSSO 1998; 2005). In 2002, the corresponding share of credit cooperatives was about 12 per cent, making commercial banks a more important of rural

---

[3] Given the change in classification of centres in 2005, the period before and after 2005 are not comparable with each other; see notes to Table A2.2.

Table A2.3 *Share of debt from formal sources in total debt of rural households, Statewise, AIDIS, 1971–2002* (per cent)

State	1971	1981	1991	2002
Maharashtra	67	86	82	85 (+)
Kerala	44	79	92	81 (−)
Himachal Pradesh	24	75	62	74 (+)
Orissa	30	81	80	74 (−)
Jammu and Kashmir	20	44	76	73 (−)
West Bengal	31	66	82	68 (−)
Gujarat	47	70	75	67 (−)
Karnataka	30	78	78	67 (−)
Madhya Pradesh	32	66	73	59 (−)
Assam	35	31	66	58 (−)
Punjab	36	74	79	56 (−)
Uttar Pradesh	23	55	69	56 (−)
Haryana	26	76	73	50 (−)
Tamil Nadu	22	44	58	47 (−)
Bihar	11	47	73	37 (−)
Rajasthan	*9*	*41*	*40*	*34 (−)*
Andhra Pradesh	14	41	34	27 (−)
All India	29	61	64	57 (−)

Note: (+)/(−)/(0) indicates increase/decrease/no change over the previous round. States are ranked in a descending order based on the figures for 2002.
Source: NSSO (1998; 2006).

credit in the State (NSSO 2005). The fall in the share of commercial banks between 1991 and 2002 corroborates the withdrawal by banks from rural areas in the 1990s. This decline in the share of formal sources was observed for the first time since the 1970s when the major Indian banks were nationalised with the objective of increasing their presence in rural areas (Table A2.3).

Between 1991 and 2002, there was also a fall in the share of rural households in Rajasthan reporting at least one outstanding debt from formal sources in general and commercial banks in particular (Table A2.4). There was, however, a rise in the percentage of households reporting at least one outstanding

Table A2.4 *Distribution of outstanding debt of rural households by source of credit, 1991 and 2002, Rajasthan and India* (per cent)

Source	Share of each source in total amount of debt			
	Rajasthan		India	
	1991	2002	1991	2002
Formal sources	36.8	33.8	64.0	57.1
Of which, commercial banks	25.4	21.0	33.7	24.5
Informal sources	55.1	66.2	32.7	42.9
Of which, moneylenders	37.3	48.9	17.6	29.6
	Percentage of households reporting at least one loan from each source			
Formal sources	13.8	12.4	15.6	13.4
Of which, commercial banks	7.9	6.9	7.5	5.7
Informal sources	18.5	23.9	9.8	15.5
Of which, moneylenders	11.3	17.7	5.4	10.1

Source: Author's calculations based on NSSO (1998; 2006).

debt from informal sources, particularly moneylenders, during this period.[4] The All India Debt and Investment Survey (AIDIS) is often criticised for an underestimation of debt (percentage of indebted households and amount of debt). However, it can be used for understanding the broad changes in terms of increase/decrease in debt indicators, as we have done here.

Information on debt profiles of rural households is available only till 2002, which is the last available round of the AIDIS.[5] However, data from the Rural Labour Enquiry (RLE) and unit-level data from the Employment–Unemployment Survey (EUS) (66th Round) of the National Sample Survey Organisation (NSSO) provide some more insight into the debt profiles of rural labour households.

Broadly, the changes in the shares of formal and informal sources reflected in the RLE and EUS are similar to those in the AIDIS. However, there is one major difference: the share of formal sources has generally been much lower for rural labour households than for rural households as a whole (Table A2.5).

---

[4] The percentage of households reporting debt from formal and informal sources may not move in opposite directions because households can borrow from more than one source.

[5] The results from the latest round of 2012–13 have just been published.

Table A2.5 *Share of debt by source, rural labour households, Rajasthan and India, RLE, 1999–2000 to 2009–10* (per cent)

Source		1999–2000	2004–05	2009–10*
Rajasthan	Formal sources	16.8	5.8	13.8
	Of which, banks	11.9	3.7	9.8
	Informal sources	83.2	96.3	86.2
	Of which, moneylenders	35.9	54.9	60.3
	All sources	100.0	100.0	100.0
India	Formal sources	35.7	29.0	36.6
	Of which, banks	17.2	16.5	21.4
	Informal sources	64.3	71.0	63.4
	Of which, moneylenders	31.7	44.2	33.1
	All sources	100.0	100.0	100.0

Note: * These figures are based on unit-level data from the Employment–Unemployment Round for this year.
Source: RBI (2008); GoI (1990; 2004; 2010); unit-level data for 2009–10.

This suggests weaker access to formal credit for rural labour households as against other segments of the rural population.

The RLE and EUS show that banks have been the most important formal source of credit for rural labour households in India as also in Rajasthan. The share of banks in the total debt of rural labour households in the State showed a decline between 1999–2000 and 2004–05. However, between 2004–05 and 2009–10, there was an increase in this share. As already noted, this was also a period of expansion in the rural branch network in Rajasthan. Yet, this did not undermine the importance of informal sources, particularly moneylenders, as sources of credit for rural labour households in the State. Moneylenders remained the largest source of credit for rural labour households, and their share in 2009–10 was in fact much higher than in 2004–05.

2

Agrarian Relations in
25 F Gulabewala

INTRODUCTION TO THE STUDY VILLAGE

25 F Gulabewala is a village in Karanpur tehsil of Sri Ganganagar district. The official name of the village is 25 F. It refers to the 25th outlet on minor canal F of the Gang Canal network from which the village receives water. When the village was settled after construction of the canal, the first residents of 25 F came from a village called Gulabewala in Punjab, and they started calling 25 F by the same name. The village is about 25 kilometres from Sri Ganganagar town on an all-weather road. The nearest railhead is at Kesarisinghpur, 9 kilometres away. The village has two primary schools and one secondary school, an Anganwadi centre, a Primary Health Centre, and a branch of the State Bank of Bikaner and Jaipur.

25 F Gulabewala is irrigated by the Gang Canal project, and as shown in Table 2.1, the entire cultivable area of the village was irrigated. There was no forest land or cultivable waste in the village. The main crops cultivated in Gulabewala were wheat, rapeseed, cotton, cluster beans and fodder crops. In recent years, a decrease in the availability of water has resulted in a decline in the cultivation of cotton. In particular, a substantial part of the agricultural land in the village is left fallow in the kharif season because of poor irrigation.

At the Census survey of 2007, there were 204 resident households in the village, and its population was 1,131 persons. The population of the village in 2001 as per the Census of India was 1,358, with 658 females and 700 males.

Table 2.2 shows the distribution of the population of the village by age-group and sex. The sex ratio was 970 females per 1,000 males. This is considerably higher than the figure for Ganganagar district, which stood at 887 in 2011, and

Table 2.1 *Land use, 25 F Gulabewala, 2007*

Land use		Area (in hectares)	As % of geographical area
Geographical are		340.00	100.0
Forest		0.00	0.0
Area under cultivation	Irrigated	300.59	88.4
	Unirrigated	0.00	0.0
Cultivable waste		0.00	0.0
Area not available for cultivation		39.41	11.6

Source: Census of India, 2001.

Table 2.2 *Distribution of population by age and sex, 25 F Gulabewala, 2007*

Age-group	Population			As percentage of corresponding total population		
	Female	Male	Persons	Female	Male	Persons
0 to < 3 years	20	29	49	3.6	5.1	4.3
3 to 6 years	32	37	69	5.7	6.5	6.1
7 to 9 years	22	32	54	3.9	5.6	4.8
10 to 14 years	63	63	126	11.3	11.0	11.1
15 to 17 years	40	47	87	7.2	8.2	7.7
18 to 24 years	82	82	164	14.7	14.3	14.5
25 to 34 years	94	83	177	16.8	14.5	15.6
35 to 49 years	97	101	198	17.4	17.6	17.5
50 to 59 years	45	38	83	8.1	6.6	7.3
60 to 69 years	34	31	65	6.1	5.4	5.7
≥ 70 years	29	30	59	5.2	5.2	5.2
All	558	573	1131	100.0	100.0	100.0

Source: Survey data.

that for rural Rajasthan, which was 932 in the same year. The child sex ratio for the age-group 0 to 6 years was much lower, however, at 788, as against 854 and 883 for Ganganagar and Rajasthan respectively in 2011.

An average household in the village comprised 5.5 persons and nearly half of all households – 45.6 per cent to be precise – had six or more members.

Of the 204 households in the village, 68 were Jat Sikh households, 60 Mazhabi Sikh (Dalit) households, 53 Nayak (Dalit Hindu) and 9 Meghwal (Dalit

Table 2.3 *Number of households, by social group, 25 F Gulabewala, 2007*

Social group	Number of households	Per cent of all households
Mazhabi Sikhs (Dalit)	60	29.4
Nayaks (Dalit)	53	25.9
Meghwals (Dalit)	9	4.4
All Dalits	*122*	*59.8*
Jat Sikhs	68	33.3
Other OBC	10	4.9
All OBC	*78*	*38.2*
Others	4	1.9
All households	204	100.0

Source: Survey data.

Hindu) households (Table 2.3). In addition to Jat Sikhs (who are classified as OBC in Rajasthan), other OBC groups in the village included Tarkhan Sikhs, Ramgadiya Sikhs, Nai Sikhs, Saini Sikhs and Kumhars. Dalits constituted the majority of households in the village.

SOCIO-ECONOMIC CLASSES

In the PARI (Project on Agrarian Relations in India) surveys, detailed socio-economic classification of households is attempted based on a combination of factors, including the level and composition of incomes, nature of labour deployment on land (including the use of family labour and wage labour), and ownership of the means of production.[1]

While classifying households in 25 F Gulabewala, first, households whose major share of income came from non-agricultural businesses or salaried jobs were separated. Households relying primarily on rents, remittances, pensions and other transfers were also separated. Of the remaining households that were dependent on agriculture, those that depended on wage labour were classified as Manual worker households. The criterion used was the contribution of wage incomes to total incomes. Given the polarisation between Manual workers, and

---

[1] For details of the broad system of classification used in PARI, see Ramachandran, Rawal and Swaminathan (2010), pp. 24–32, and Ramachandran (2011).

landowners and cultivators (see below), this categorisation was not difficult in 25 F Gulabewala.[2]

Among the households that cultivated land, four classes were identified, based primarily on the value of ownership of means of production.

(i) Landlords and/or big capitalist farmers 1: households whose total value of means of production was over Rs 150 lakhs. There were seven households in this class. These households had the largest ownership and operational holdings in the village. They also held the bulk of agricultural machinery. Members of these households did not participate in major manual operations on the land that they cultivated.

(ii) Landlords and/or big capitalist farmers 2: households whose means of production were valued at more than Rs 80 lakhs but less than Rs 150 lakhs per household, or who held operational holdings of more than 50 acres each.

(iii) Farmers 1: households that owned and operated land, and had productive assets valued between Rs 30 and 80 lakhs.

(iv) Farmers 2: households that owned and operated land, but with productive assets valued at less than Rs 30 lakhs.

The extent of capitalist development of agriculture was high in Gulabewala, as revealed by the data on use of wage labour vis-à-vis family labour. While no member of the Landlords and/or big capitalist farmers 1 group engaged in any family labour, the ratio of family labour to wage labour was very low for all classes of cultivators (Table 2.4).

The average labour ratio (ratio of labour-days worked by members of the household to labour-days hired by the household) was highest for Farmers 2 households, but even here the ratio was very low. Further, no person from any of the four landowning cultivator classes participated in wage labour.

The distribution of households by socio-economic class is shown in Table 2.5. The largest class, consisting of 114 households or 56 per cent of all households, was of Manual workers. Farmers classified into four categories comprised a total of 58 households or 28 per cent of all households. Thirty-two households were engaged in non-agricultural occupations and categorised into three different classes.

A striking feature of the economy of 25 F Gulabewala was the association

---

[2] By contrast, in some villages, it is very difficult to draw the line between Manual workers and poor peasants (Dhar 2013).

Table 2.4 *Average labour ratio (ratio of labour-days worked by members of the household to labour-days hired by the household) for socio-economic classes that operated land, by socio-economic class, 25 F Gulabewala, 2006–07*

Socio-economic class	Labour ratio
Landlords and/or big capitalist farmers 1	0
Landlords and/or big capitalist farmers 2	0.11
Farmers 1	0.31
Farmers 2	0.9

Source: Survey data.

Table 2.5 *Number and proportion of households, by socio-economic class, 25 F Gulabewala, 2006–07*

Socio-economic class	Households	Per cent of all households
Landlords and/or big capitalist farmers 1	7	3.4
Landlords and/or big capitalist farmers 2	13	6.3
Farmers 1	26	12.7
Farmers 2	12	5.9
Manual workers	114	56.0
Business activity/self-employed	12	5.9
Salaried persons	10	4.9
Receives rents, remittances, pensions, handouts	10	4.9
All	204	100

Source: Survey data.

between caste (or social group) and class (Table 2.6). All the cultivator households except one were Jat Sikhs, and the majority of Dalit households – 56 out of 60 Mazhabi Sikh households and 55 out of 62 Nayak Dalit households – were Manual workers. With one exception, Manual worker households neither owned nor operated agricultural land (except one household, which had 1.6 acres of land). Among the four classes of farmer households, the smallest operational holding was 6.08 acres and the largest holding was 310.72 acres.

Table 2.6 *Number of households, by social group and socio-economic class, 25 F Gulabewala, 2007*

Socio-economic class	Jat Sikh (OBC)	Other OBC	Mazhabi Sikh (Dalit)	Other Dalit	Others	Total
Landlords and/or big capitalist farmers 1	7	0	0	0	0	7
Landlords and/or big capitalist farmers 2	13	0	0	0	0	13
Farmers 1	26	0	0	0	0	26
Farmers 2	11	0	1	0	0	12
Manual workers	0	2	56	55	1	114
Business activity/self-employed	0	5	1	4	2	12
Salaried persons	3	2	1	3	1	10
Receives rents, remittances, pensions, handouts	8	1	1	0	0	10
All	68	10	60	62	4	204

Source: Survey data.

LITERACY AND EDUCATION

Rajasthan's record in terms of progress in levels of literacy and educational attainment is poor. As per the 2011 Census, only 55.3 per cent of rural women and 75.9 per cent of rural men in Sri Ganganagar district were literate (Census of India 2013). Data on literacy and educational attainments from the survey in 25 F Gulabewala show not only low overall levels of literacy and educational attainments, but also sharp class, caste and gender disparities in educational attainments.[3]

In the PARI survey, respondents were categorised in terms of literacy, not in a binary manner as literate/non-literate but into four categories – 'cannot read or write', 'can only sign name', 'can read but not write', 'can read and write' – and it is only the last category that we treat as literate in the discussion that follows.

Overall literacy rates for persons above the age of 7 was 47.8 for women and 60 per cent for men (Table 2.7). The variation in literacy rates across socio-

---

[3] A detailed discussion of issues related to deprivation in access to schooling and educational attainment in 25 F Gulabewala can be found in FAS (2012).

Table 2.7 *Proportion of literates in the population (7 years and above), by sex and socio-economic class, 25 F Gulabewala, 2007*

Socio-economic class	Women	Men	Persons
Landlords and/or big capitalist farmers 1	71.9	94.9	84.5
Landlords and/or big capitalist farmers 2	66.7	73.9	70.6
Farmers 1	69.2	90.8	79.9
Farmers 2	64.3	70.0	67.2
Manual workers	31.9	37.1	34.5
Business activity/self-employed	69.2	81.0	74.5
Salaried persons	40.7	74.2	58.6
Receives rents, remittances, pensions, handouts	52.6	68.8	60.0
All households	47.8	60.0	53.9

Source: Survey data.

Table 2.8 *Proportion of literates in the population (7 years and above), by sex and social group, 25 F Gulabewala, 2007*

Social group	Women	Men
Dalits	32.3	39.6
OBC	67.0	82.7
Others	66.7	87.5
All	47.8	60

Note: OBC category includes Jat Sikh households.
Source: Survey data.

economic classes was high. Less than 40 per cent of Manual workers, men and women, were literate. Among Landlords and/or big capitalist farmers 1, 95 per cent men and 72 per cent women were literate.

This inequality was also reflected in literacy by social group (Table 2.8). Among Dalit men, only 40 per cent were literate. Among Jat Sikh and other OBC men, 83 per cent were literate.

Educational Attainment

To assess the educational achievements of the population, first, for those above the age of 16 years, we computed the median years of schooling completed. The

Table 2.9 *Median number of completed years of schooling for population above 16 years, by sex and socio-economic class, 25 F Gulabewala, 2007*

Socio-economic class	Women	Men	Persons
Landlords and/or big capitalist farmers 1	7	10	9
Landlords and/or big capitalist farmers 2	8	9	8
Farmers 1	8	9	8
Farmers 2	5	8	5
Manual workers	0	0	0
Business activity/self-employed	7	10	8
Salaried persons	0	7	5
Receives rents, remittances, pensions, handouts	0	4	3
All households	0	5	2

Source: Survey data.

Table 2.10 *Median number of completed years of schooling for population above 16 years, by sex and social group, 25 F Gulabewala, 2007*

Social group	Female	Male	Persons
Dalits	0	0	0
OBC	6	9	8
Others	8	9	8
All	0	5	2

Note: OBC category includes Jat Sikh households.
Source: Survey data.

median was found to be 0 for men and women from Manual worker households (Table 2.9). Men from landowning farming households had 8 to 10 years of schooling. Again, the inequality across social groups was high, with 0 median year of schooling among Dalit men and women (Table 2.10).

Next, we counted the number of persons who had obtained a college degree, which requires, at a minimum, fifteen completed years of schooling. For this exercise, we confined ourselves to the population aged 25 years or more. There were 30 graduates or degree-holders in Gulabewala village, but only 1 of them was from a Scheduled Caste household (Table 2.12). Overall, only around 5 per cent of persons aged 25 years or older were graduates, the figure being

Table 2.11 *Graduates in the age-group 25 years and above, by socio-economic class and sex, 25 F Gulabewala, 2007*

Socio-economic class	Number		Per cent	
	Women	Men	Women	Men
Landlords and/or big capitalist farmers 1	2	6	6.1	20.7
Landlords and/or big capitalist farmers 2	2	4	3.5	8.3
Farmers 1	1	1	5.6	5.3
Farmers 2	0	0	0	0
Manual workers	0	0	0	0
Business activity/self-employed	2	5	13.3	35.7
Salaried persons	0	0	0	0
Receives rents, remittances, pensions, handouts	0	0	0	0
All households	9	21	3	7.4

Source: Survey data.

Table 2.12 *Graduates in the age-group 25 years and above, by social group and sex, 25 F Gulabewala, 2007*

Social group	Number		Per cent	
	Women	Men	Women	Men
Dalits	0	1	0	0.7
OBC	8	19	5.1	13.5
Others	1	1	14.3	16.7
All	9	21	3	7.4

Note: OBC category includes Jat Sikh households.
Source: Survey data.

even lower for females, at 3 per cent. There was no graduate among Manual worker households (Table 2.11).

School Attendance

All three aspects of the challenge of universal school education – enrolment, retention and achievement with regard to learning outcomes – remain unmet in India. In the more backward parts of the country, universal enrolment and attendance constitute the primary challenges. The data on school

Table 2.13 *Number and proportion of children attending school, by age-group and sex, 25 F Gulabewala, 2007*

Age-group	Number of children			As percentage of all children		
	Female	Male	Persons	Female	Male	Persons
6 to 10 years	38	50	88	82.6	89.3	86.3
11 to 14 years	27	40	67	57.4	81.6	69.8
15 to 16 years	14	20	34	56.0	62.5	59.6
17 to 18 years	12	11	23	34.3	35.5	34.8
6 to 18 years	91	121	212	59.5	72.0	66.0

Source: FAS (2012).

Table 2.14 *Gross enrolment ratio of children, by level of schooling, by sex, 25 F Gulabewala, 2007*

School level	Number enrolled			GER		
	Female	Male	Persons	Female	Male	Persons
Standard I to V	52	65	117	102.0	94.2	97.5
Standard VI to VIII	23	33	56	48.9	67.4	58.3
Standard IX to X	14	12	26	35.9	25.5	30.2
Standard XI to XII	4	11	15	8.9	23.9	16.5

Note: Gross enrolment ratio (GER) is defined as the total enrolment in the specific level of education, irrespective of age, expressed as a percentage of the official school-age population, corresponding to the same level of education in a given school year. The Annual Report of the Ministry of Human Resource Development (MHRD), India, 2008–09 provides data on GER for three school levels. The corresponding school age for the three levels specified by the MHRD are as follows: Standard I to V: 6 to 11 years; Standard VI to VIII: 11 to 14 years; Standard IX to XII: 14 to 18 years. In the Table, we have divided Standard IX to XII further into two categories: Standard IX to X: 14 to 16 years; Standard XI to XII: 16 to 18 years
Source: FAS (2012), p. 26.

attendance presented in Table 2.13 and that on gross enrolment ratios presented in Table 2.14 show that 25 F Gulabewala has quite some distance still to go, to achieve universal school enrolment and attendance. These data are for children up to the age of 18, the cut-off used internationally to define an adult.

Overall attendance ratios were well below 100 per cent even in the age-group of 6 to 10 years, and significantly lower for girls as compared to boys in the age-group of 11 to 14 years. Attendance rates for boys declined sharply after

16 years. Only around a third of boys and girls in the age-group of 17–18 years were attending school.

The attendance ratios were substantially lower for children belonging to Scheduled Castes than for Other Backward Classes in all age-groups, and for both boys and girls (Tables 2.15 and 2.16).

The gross enrolment ratios (GER) were also unimpressive. Enrolment ratios declined sharply for girls beyond primary school and for boys after middle school. About 40 per cent of girls and 28 per cent of boys in the age-group 6–18 years did not go to school (Table 2.13). School attendance rates dropped sharply after the primary-school-going age. While about 83 per cent of girls in the age-group 6–14 years went to school, the proportion of school-going children dropped to 57 per cent among girls aged 11–14 years, and dropped further when one looked at older children. Only 34 per cent girls in the age-group 17–18 years went to school.

Table 2.15 *Boys attending school, by age-group and social group, 25 F Gulabewala, 2007*

Age-group	Dalit		OBC	
	Number	Per cent	Number	Per cent
6 to 10 years	30	83.3	18	100.0
11 to 14 years	13	61.9	27	96.4
15 to 16 years	9	42.9	11	100.0
17 to 18 years	1	5.6	10	76.9
6 to 18 years	53	55.2	66	94.3

Source: Survey data.

Table 2.16 *Girls attending school, by age-group and social group, 25 F Gulabewala, 2007*

Age-group	Dalit		OBC	
	Number	Per cent	Number	Per cent
6 to 10 years	31	79.5	7	100.0
11 to 14 years	21	52.5	6	85.7
15 to 16 years	5	31.3	9	100.0
17 to 18 years	4	17.4	8	66.7
6 to 18 years	61	51.7	30	85.7

Source: Survey data.

Table 2.17 *Proportion of girls and boys attending school,*
by age-group, Manual worker households, 25 F Gulabewala, 2007

Age-group	Girls	Boys
6–10 years	77.8	82.9
11–14 years	51.4	57.1
15–16 years	31.3	42.9
17–18 years	13.0	5.9
6–18 years	50.9	45.7

Source: Survey data.

The drop-out rate was particularly sharp for children from Manual worker and Dalit households. Only 17.4 per cent of Dalit girls and 5.6 per cent of Dalit boys in the age-group 17–18 years went to school (Tables 2.15 and 2.16).

Among children from Manual worker households, a group that comprised 56 per cent of the population, rates of school attendance were low even among the younger age-groups. Around one-half of boys and girls aged 11 to 14 were not attending school. Attendance rates among older children were even lower: among 17–18-year-old children from Manual worker households, only 13 per cent of girls and 5.9 per cent of boys were in school (Table 2.17). As the next section shows, many of these out-of-school children were engaged in work.

Child Labour

In India, there is a legal provision that children below the age of 14 completed years are not to be engaged in certain occupations. There is also legislation now that requires children up to the age of 14 to be enrolled in and attending an educational institution. In reality, however, not all children aged 14 years or younger are in school.

In Gulabewala, a rather high proportion of children aged between 6 and 14 years – nearly one-fifth – were working children.[4] Most of them – more than a fifth of all girls and over one-tenth of all boys – were in fact working for an employer outside the household, while a relatively small percentage were working on the household operational holding.

---

[4] 'Work' here refers to paid or unpaid work outside the household for an employer, work on household operational holding, and work in any household enterprise other than that relating to animal resources. Children engaged in any of these activities are working children.

Of the 32 children working for an employer outside the household, all the girls and all but one of the boys belonged to the Scheduled Castes. At the same time, more than one-sixth of boys and more than one-fourth of girls aged 6 to 14 years from Scheduled Caste households in Gulabewala were working, all of them as wage labourers. Box 1 describes some of the child workers in Gulabewala.

BOX 1: Child Workers

We give below a brief description of four households with regular child workers, as observed at the time of the survey.

1. Kuldeep, aged 12 years, is a long-term worker for a big landlord. He comes from a Scheduled Caste family. His father met with a road accident some years ago and is unable to work. His mother is engaged as a domestic worker, and his younger brother is at school. The family has no land, and even the house they live in has been given to them by the landlord.

Kuldeep began working at the age of 10. He works from 7 am to 7 pm every day at various tasks related to animal husbanding and housework in the landlord's house. Last year, his earnings were Rs 6,667 in cash; he was given two meals and tea at the landlord's house every day.

2. Dinar is a 70-year-old man whose two sons and two daughters live with him. The eldest daughter was married but is now separated, and lives with her three children in her father's household. She works as a domestic worker for a big landowning family, and also participates in agricultural labour. Her three children are in school. Both Dinar's sons, aged 16 and 14, are long-term workers. His fourth child, a daughter, also works as a domestic employee, and participates in agricultural and non-agricultural employment. The family is landless, belongs to the Meghwal caste (Dalit) and had migrated to Gulabewala in 1965.

Both boys work the year round for big landlord families. Their tasks pertain mainly to animal husbandry and domestic work. The elder boy, K, earned Rs 10,000 the previous year. His original contract was for 12,000 but as he was ill and did not work for two months, he was paid less. K works for 9 to 10 hours a day and performs the following tasks: cleaning the house, washing clothes, cleaning utensils, clearing the dung, feeding the animals, cutting fodder, and carrying food for the workers in the field.

The younger boy, S, was due to receive Rs 6000 but was paid Rs 4500, as he too fell ill for a few days. His wage is lower as he is younger, the father said. Although he performs the same tasks as his elder brother, he is said to be 'less efficient' by his employer.

The family has taken loans from both landlords, and thus remain tied to the employers.

3. Sarati, a widow, lives with four children aged 7 to 15. Her husband was an alcoholic and committed suicide a few months prior to the survey. The family has no land and belongs to the Meghwal caste (Dalit). The eldest son, aged 15 and mentally challenged, spends his days grazing animals. Two daughters, aged 13 and 14, are both domestic employees in the same household where the mother works. All three (mother and daughters) work for a big capitalist farmer (owning 48 acres of land), and their tasks cover all the work of the household as well as care of the animals. The combined wage received by the mother and two daughters was Rs 500 the previous year. In addition, all three were given *roti*s and a glass of milk once a day. Originally, they were to be paid Rs 2,000 in cash, but as the family took some wheat and old clothes, the cash payment was lessened.

4. A young agricultural-labourer couple live with their four daughters (aged 10 to 14) and son (aged 8). The son and one daughter attend school, but the other three girls are all working. The girls work at a variety of agricultural tasks such as cotton-picking, harvesting wheat and green gram, and also help with household chores.

Comment: The experiences of these four households where childen, both girls and boys, have been engaged in hard manual labour from a young age reflect the extreme poverty and vulnerability of landless Scheduled Caste families of Gulabewala. As the last case study indicates, even with both parents working as full-time agricultural labourers, the children have been drawn into the work force. In the other three cases, the death or disability of an adult male worker was a further factor that forced young children to work.

These case studies demonstrate that the availability of a government school in the neighbourhood is far from adequate to ensure that all children attend school. Free books, uniforms, shoes and generous scholarships are needed to ensure universal school attendance.

Source: FAS (2012), pp. 19–20.

LAND AND WEALTH INEQUALITY

The village of 25 F Gulabewala was characterised by an extremely high degree of inequality in ownership of land and other assets. The incidence of landlessness was very high: 65 per cent of households in the village did not own any agricultural land.

If we group households by decile of land owned, we find that the top 10 per cent of households owned 61 per cent of land and cultivated 66 per cent of total operational holdings (Table 2.18). By contrast, the lowest 60 per cent of households together owned less than 1 per cent of the total land.

In our survey, we collected data on assets other than land including buildings, trees, livestock and other animals, means of production, means of transport, and other assets including household durables. If we examine the distribution of wealth or total assets, a similar concentration is observed. The top 10 per cent of households accounted for 61 per cent of total wealth, and the richest 30 per cent of households accounted for 97.5 per cent of total wealth. In other words, the poorest 70 per cent of the population owned only 2.5 per cent of

Table 2.18 *Distribution of ownership holding of land, operational holding of land and wealth across deciles of households, 25 F Gulabewala* (per cent)

Decile	Share in ownership holding	Share in operational holding	Share in total wealth
1	0	0	0.02
2	0	0	0.07
3	0	0	0.10
4	0	0	0.13
5	0	0	0.17
6	0	0	0.28
7	2	0	1.81
8	13	10	11.31
9	24	24	24.29
10	61	66	61.83
All	100	100	100.00

Note: For each column, the ranking of households into deciles is based on the selected variable (that is, ownership holding or operational holding or total wealth).
Source: Survey data.

Table 2.19 *Distribution of ownership holding of land and wealth across socio-economic classes, and Access Index, 25 F Gulabewala* (per cent)

Socio-economic class	House-holds (%)	Land owned (%)	Access Index (land)	Wealth (%)	Access Index (wealth)
Landlords and/or big capitalist farmers 1	3	33	9.76	35	10.3
Landlords and/or big capitalist farmers 2	6	27	4.16	25	3.85
Farmers 1	13	28	2.24	28	2.17
Farmers 2	6	4	0.71	4	0.62
Manual workers	56	0	0	1	0.02
Business activity/self-employed	6	0	0.03	0.4	0.06
Salaried person/s	5	2	0.31	1	0.25
Receives rents, remittances, pensions, handouts	5	6	1.18	5.6	1.29
All households	100	100	1.00	100	1.00

Note: The Access Index is defined as the ratio of the share of the ith class in total land/wealth to the share of the ith class in population.
Source: Survey data.

Table 2.20 *Distribution of ownership holding of land and wealth across social groups, and Access Index, 25 F Gulabewala* (per cent)

Social group	Households (%)	Land owned (%)	Access Index (land)	Wealth (%)	Access Index (wealth)
Mazhabi Sikhs (Dalits)	29.4	0.2	0.01	0.7	0.02
Other Dalits	30.9	0.1	0	0.4	0.01
Jat Sikhs	33.3	99.5	2.99	98.0	2.94
All households	100	100	1.00	100	1.00

Note: The Access Index is defined as the ratio of the share of the ith class in total land/wealth to the share of the ith class in population.
Source: Survey data.

the wealth of all resident households. The Access Index, a measure of relative inequality, was as high as 10 for Landlords and/or big capitalist farmers 1, and as low as 0.02 for Manual workers. A ratio of 1 indicates that the selected class owns assets proportional to its share in the population.

We now turn to patterns of land and wealth ownership across socio-economic classes. Landlords and/or big capitalist farmers 1, Landlords and/or big capitalist farmers 2, and Farmers 1 together accounted for 21 per cent of households, and owned 88 per cent of land and 88 per cent of wealth (Table 2.19). By contrast, the class of Manual workers, which accounted for 56 per cent of households, owned only 1 per cent of total wealth.

As noted earlier, there was almost perfect overlap between caste and class. Jat Sikh households constituted about one-third of all households, but owned and operated almost all the land and accounted for 98 per cent of total wealth (Table 2.20). Dalit and other OBC households were almost entirely landless.

Composition of Assets

If we examine the composition of total assets or wealth, it is clear that agricultural land is the most valuable asset for households in Gulabewala village. The mean value of agricultural land was Rs 62.75 lakhs and the median value Rs 45 lakhs (Table 2.21), taking all households together. As more than 50 per cent of households did not own land, it is not surprising that the median value of assets was as low as Rs 2,000. To put it differently, the household in the 50th position on a ranking of assets in the village owned assets worth Rs 2,000.

There were stark differences in asset ownership across socio-economic classes (Table 2.22). The average farmer household owned Rs 92.61 lakhs of

Table 2.21 *Median and mean values of different assets, all households, 25 F Gulabewala, 2007* (Rs)

Categories of assets	Median value of assets	Average value of assets
Land and water bodies (including trees), of which	20,000	713,829
Agricultural land	4500,000	6275,169
Homestead land, houses and other buildings	25,000	132,471
Animals and livestock (including draught animals)	3,800	13,332
Means of production	5,000	21,736
Means of transport	1,000	22,303
Domestic durable goods	800	2,037
Other assets (inventories)	2,450	19,284
All assets	2,000	129,620

Source: Survey data.

Table 2.22 *Average values of assets in different asset categories, by selected socio-economic class, 25 F Gulabewala, 2007 (Rs)*

Socio-economic class	Land and water bodies (including trees)	Houses, homestead land, any other land and buildings	Animals and livestock (including draught animals)	Means of production	Means of transport	Domestic durable goods	Other assets (inventories)	All assets
Landlords and/or big capitalist farmers 1 and 2, Farmers 1 and 2	7794,389	949,894	84,225	259,286	60,196	55,859	95,706	9261,073
Manual workers	8089	42,005	5395	706	599	2642	1299	46,608
All households	4769,813	366,363	34,168	169,399	32,712	21,538	33,888	2889,131

Source: Survey data.

assets, as compared to Rs 46,608 for the average Manual worker household (or a ratio of almost 200:1). While agricultural land was the most valuable component of the assets of landlords and farmers, they also owned non-agricultural land, livestock and machinery of substantial value. However, for Manual workers, the value of their house and homestead was the most important component of total assets (see also Appendix Tables A1.1 and A1.2).

IRRIGATION AND CROPPING PATTERN

Land in 25 F Gulabewala was irrigated by the minor canal F of the Gang Canal (Bikaner Canal) system. The Gang Canal, built in 1927, was originally designed to be fed with water from the Sutlej river at the Hussainiwala Head Works (+30° 59' 28"N, +74° 33' 6"E), and to irrigate parts of what was then Bikaner State. From the 1960s, after completion of the Harike Barrage (+31° 8' 46"N, +74° 56' 46"E) at the confluence of the Sutlej and Beas rivers, upstream of Hussainiwala Head Works, the Bikaner Canal is fed by water from the Harike Barrage (via Ferozepur Feeder and Sirhind Feeder canals) (see Figure 2.1).

The command area of the Gang Canal was divided into a grid of segments called *chaks*, and, in most cases, one village was settled in each *chak*. Each *chak* was provided irrigation by a separate outlet in the distributory canal that serviced it. Agricultural land in 25 F Gulabewala was irrigated by the 25th outlet of the minor canal F of the Gang Canal system. Irrigation water from the canal reached each plot of land through a network of field channels designed to irrigate plots of land one by one, by rotation. In a cycle of watering, each plot of land was entitled to irrigation for a specified duration, in proportion to the area of land. Each plot received water at a pre-notified time of day or night, a schedule that was changed periodically.

Almost all the land cultivated by households in the village (including the land they cultivated outside the village) was canal-irrigated (Table 2.23). However, water available from the canal was not sufficient for irrigating the entire operational holdings, particularly in the kharif season.[5] Hence farmers were allowed to combine water rights (in terms of minutes of watering) for different plots operated by them and to use the water on any set of plots. Some farmers even took land on lease to be able to utilise the water rights on leased-

---

[5] The requirement of irrigation water during the kharif season was high in 25 F Gulabewala because of very high summer temperatures and sandy soils with low water retention capacity.

Figure 2.1 *Canals of the Gang Canal network through which irrigation water reaches 25 F Gulabewala*

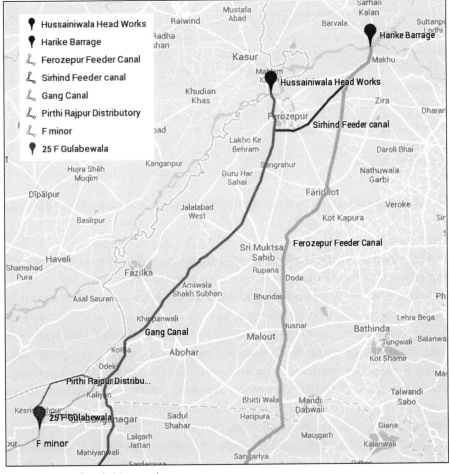

Prepared using Google Maps engine.

in land on their own land, while the leased land was left fallow. In addition, farmers used private tubewells to augment canal irrigation.

Inadequacy of water supplied by the canal made access to groundwater of critical importance. However, given the salinity of groundwater, it could be used only to a limited extent. Limited supply of electricity also constrained the extent to which tubewells could be deployed for irrigation. Until 2006–07, only a few farmers had built water-storage tanks on their land; this allowed them

Table 2.23 *Area irrigated by different sources, 25 F Gulabewala, in acres and as per cent of total operational holdings*

Sources of irrigation	Extent (acres)	Per cent of total operational holding
Canal	2526	99
Tubewell	1796	70
Unirrigated	9	0
Total operational holding	2552	100

Note: Column 3 does not add up to 100 as each plot can have more than one source of irrigation.
Source: Survey data.

to pump groundwater when electricity was supplied and store it for use later.[6] About 70 per cent of land in 25 F Gulabewala had some access to irrigation from tubewells.

On account of the inadequacy of irrigation, only about 37 per cent of operational holdings of land were cultivated in the kharif season. The cropping pattern in the survey year is shown in Table 2.24. American cotton, sown on 27 per cent of the operational holdings, was the most important crop cultivated during this season.[7] In 2006–07, about 6 per cent of operated land was sown with cluster beans in the kharif season. Cluster beans require very little water and was therefore particularly suitable given the scarcity of irrigation during the kharif season.[8] In the rabi season, rapeseed, which accounted for 42 per cent of the operated land, and wheat, which accounted for 32 per cent of the operated land, were the two important crops.

Table 2.25 shows that average yields of major crops in 25 F Gulabewala were higher than the corresponding average yields in Rajasthan as a whole and in India.

---

[6] Many farmers in 25 F Gulabewala built field-level tanks after 2007–08 using subsidies provided by the State government for the purpose.

[7] Transgenic varieties of cotton were not sown in 25 F Gulabewala until 2011–12.

[8] The extent of cultivation of cluster beans has increased in recent years in 25 F Gulabewala because of high industrial demand for gum made from cluster beans, which resulted in a sharp increase in prices of cluster beans. Between 2006–07 and 2010–11, area sown with cluster beans in Sri Ganganagar district as a whole increased by about 43,000 hectares, an increase of about 36 per cent over this period.

Table 2.24 *Area under different crops as a proportion of total operational holding and gross cropped area* (per cent)

Season	Crop	Share in gross cropped area	Share in total land operated
Kharif	American cotton	21	27
Kharif	Cluster beans	5	6
Kharif	Fodder crops	2	3
Kharif	Other kharif crops	1	2
Kharif	All kharif crops	30	37
Rabi	Rapeseed	34	42
Rabi	Wheat	26	32
Rabi	Barley	5	7
Rabi	Fodder crops	2	3
Rabi	Other rabi crops	2	3
Rabi	All rabi crops	69	86
Annual	All annual crops	1	1
All	All crops	100	124

Source: Survey data.

Table 2.25 *Average yield of main crops, 25 F Gulabewala, Rajasthan and India* (kg per acre)

	American cotton	Cluster beans	Rapeseed	Wheat
25 F Gulabewala	672	384	577	1449
Sri Ganganagar	145		552	1441
Rajasthan	147		480	1113
India	170		443	1096

Source: Survey data; Directorate of Economics and Statistics, Ministry of Agriculture, Government of India.

COST OF CULTIVATION AND INCOME FROM CROP PRODUCTION

For each crop and each operational holding, we have calculated the gross value of output and costs of cultivation. The cost concept used is close to cost A2 of the Commission on Agricultural Costs and Prices (CACP). In this study, the following costs are included in cost A2:

- Value of seed (farm-produced and purchased)
- Value of manure (farm-produced and purchased)
- Value of fertilizers
- Recurrent cost of irrigation (rental costs, fuel costs, water charges)
- Value of plant protection chemicals
- Hired human labour
- Recurrent cost of deploying animals (hired and owned)
- Recurrent cost of deploying machines (hired and owned)
- Rent for leased-in land
- Interest on working capital
- Depreciation of owned fixed capital
- Land revenue and other taxes
- Crop insurance
- Marketing expenses
- Maintenance cost of owned machinery
- Other miscellaneous expenses.

Cost A2, broadly speaking, refers to paid-out costs. It does not include any imputed value of family labour or any imputed rental value of owned fixed capital (including land).

Net incomes are defined as GVO (gross value of output) minus cost A2. In terms of the entire operational holding of a cultivator household, the GVO averaged around Rs 13,000 an acre or Rs 31,944 per hectare. After adjusting for paid-out costs, net incomes averaged Rs 6,500 per acre or Rs 16,070 per hectare. In comparison to other villages surveyed under PARI, gross and net incomes from cultivation are relatively high in Gulabewala.

Recent studies on returns from farming have shown that a significant proportion of cultivator households incur losses in crop production (Ramachandran, Rawal and Swaminathan 2010; Rawal 2013; Swaminathan and Rawal 2011). In 25 F Gulabewala, no household incurred a loss in crop production during 2006–07 (Rawal 2013). However, there were clear variations across socio-economic classes. The GVO ranged from an average of Rs 11,890 per acre for Farmers 2 households to Rs 18,415 per acre for Landlords and/or big capitalist farmers 1 households (Table 2.26). After deducting costs, net incomes were close to Rs 10,000 an acre for the Landlords and/or big capitalist farmers 1 group and Rs 6,679 for the Farmers 2 group (the smallest category of farmers). To put it differently, the return per hectare was Rs 23,872 for Landlords and/or

Table 2.26 *Average gross value of output, cost A2 and net income from crop production, by class, 25 F Gulabewala* (Rs per acre)

Socio-economic class	Gross value of output	Cost A2	Net income
Landlords and/or big capitalist farmers 1	18415	8751	9665
Landlords and/or big capitalist farmers 2	12925	6840	6085
Farmers 1	13323	6370	6952
Farmers 2	11890	5212	6679
Salaried persons	10448	6186	4262
Receives rents, remittances, pensions, handouts	6749	5411	1337
All households	12933	6427	6506

Source: Survey data.

Table 2.27 *Average gross value of output, cost A2 and net income from different crops, 25 F Gulabewala* (Rs per acre)

Crop	25 F Gulabewala			Irrigated North-Western (INW) Plain region (CCPC estimates)		
	Gross value of output	Cost A2	Net income	Gross value of output	Cost A2	Net income
American cotton	12381	7613	4768	13115	3065	10050
Cluster beans	7101	3392	3709	–	–	–
Green gram	7482	3368	4115	7519	1479	6040
Rapeseed	10703	4383	6320	10673	1795	8878
Wheat*	13329	6034	7295	18157	3901	14256
Barley	7896	4144	3751	11064	2759	8305
Gram	10694	4787	5907	7618	2116	5501
Sugarcane	29250	19242	10008	–	–	–

Note: * Data for wheat for the INW Plain region refer to 2007–08, as CCPC data for wheat were not available for the region for 2006–07.
Source: Estimated using CCPC data.

big capitalist farmers 1 households and Rs 16,497 for Farmers 2 households. This systematic variation in net incomes has been observed in almost all the PARI surveys (see Rawal and Swaminathan 2013).

The inverse farm-size profitability argument, advanced by some scholars, states that small farmers get a higher return per acre as compared to large farmers. Our analysis of gross and net incomes from cultivation across socio-economic classes (rather than farm-size in terms of acreage) clearly shows a positive relationship between scale of production and income from crop production. The big capitalist farmer operates on a larger scale and makes a higher income per acre than the smaller farmer.

Turning to crop-wise returns, Table 2.27 shows that net incomes from rabi crops – wheat, rapeseed and gram – were higher than returns from kharif crops in 25 F Gulabewala. Returns were also high for sugarcane, a longer-duration crop. Table 2.27 also shows corresponding estimates, from the CCPC surveys, of average returns for the Irrigated North-Western (INW) Plains region. It is seen that estimates of average value of output from the CCPC survey for the region and the PARI survey for 25 F Gulabewala are very similar. However, there is a big difference between the CCPC estimate and the PARI village survey in terms of cost of production. The PARI survey estimates of costs of

Table 2.28 *Average expenditure on different items in cultivation of major crops, 25 F Gulabewala* (Rs per acre)

Item	American cotton	Cluster beans	Green gram	Rapeseed	Wheat
Seed material	209	174	238	40	487
Manure	120	0	0	123	19
Chemical fertilizer	707	231	239	540	943
Plant protection chemicals	1568	194	130	84	111
Irrigation	364	289	164	385	449
Casual labour	1401	432	477	360	723
Long-term labour	325	267	262	323	386
Machines	1357	1076	1136	1347	1544
Draught animals	0	0	0	0	0
Rent for leased-in land	477	225	74	411	449
Other crop-specific expenses	149	54	36	100	135
Annual expenses	0	0	0	0	0
Cost A2	7613	3392	3368	4383	6034

Source: Survey data.

cultivation in 25 F Gulabewala are much higher than costs for the same crop estimated by CCPC for the entire INW Plains region of Rajasthan. While the regional picture may differ from that of a single village for a variety of reasons, we believe that the CCPC is likely to have underestimated costs.[9]

Detailed accounts of the costs incurred are shown in Table 2.28. Although the gross value of output from cultivation of American cotton in the kharif season was high, the net returns were low on account of high costs of cultivation. Cotton cultivation resulted in high expenditure on chemicals as well as on casual labour (for cotton-picking). The average cost incurred in the cultivation of American cotton was Rs 7,613 per acre, or more than double the cost of cultivation of cluster beans and of green gram.

Table 2.29 shows comparable estimates of average costs on different items for the INW Plain region from the CCPC surveys. A comparison of Table 2.28 and Table 2.29 suggests that the CCPC surveys hugely underestimate costs on

Table 2.29 *Average expenditure on different items in cultivation of major crops, Irrigated North Western (INW) Plains region, 2006–07* (Rs per acre)

Item	Cotton	Green gram	Mustard and Rapeseed	Wheat*
Seed material	188	305	63	712
Manure	13	0	0	312
Chemical fertilizer	435	0	323	513
Plant protection chemicals	702	30	21	35
Irrigation	112	29	71	386
Casual labour	102	69	80	152
Long-term labour	234	125	111	79
Machines	481	371	695	1002
Draught animals	317	236	178	241
Rent for leased-in land	132	160	0	170
Other expenses	349	154	253	299
Cost A2	3065	1479	1795	3901

Note: Data for wheat refer to 2007–08 as data for wheat were not available for the region from CCPC surveys for 2006–07.

Source: Estimated using unit-level data from CCPC surveys (Rawal 2014).

[9] For more on the CCPC methodology, see Sen and Bhatia (2004).

BOX 2: Farm Harvest Price and MSP

We computed the weighted average farm harvest price (FHP) of wheat in Gulabewala and compared it with the minimum support price (MSP) offered. Farm harvest prices varied from Rs 675 per quintal to Rs 900 per quintal. The average FHP was Rs 861 for 100 kg of wheat in Gulabewala in 2006–07, higher than the announced support price of Rs 650 that year. Further, all wheat producers in Gulabewala received prices higher than the MSP announced by the central government.

The FHP was higher than the centrally announced MSP of wheat in Gulabewala mainly for two reasons: (a) the Rajasthan State government had been announcing a bonus for most of the year over the central MSP; and (b) the prevailing market price of wheat in Rajasthan was higher than the centrally announced MSP. It is interesting to note here that the gap between the MSP of wheat and the market price of wheat was so high in 2006–07 in Rajasthan that even after announcing bonuses on MSP, the government could not procure wheat from the market (India Budget 2007–08).

Data on costs of cultivation (Graph 1 below) show that MSP covered costs (A2 + FL) for almost all cultivators. The costs of producing 100 kg of wheat varied across cultivators, from Rs 164 to Rs 916. It is also evident from CCPC data that the centrally announced MSP (Rs 650) was higher than the State average cost of production (Rs 588 per quintal in 2006–07).

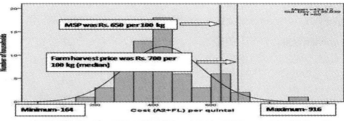

Graph 1 Distribution of Cost (A2+FL) per 100 kg of Wheat in 25F Gulabewala, Rajasthan, 2006-07

As market prices were higher than MSP, the Rajasthan State government announced a bonus on MSP in order to ensure procurement (a policy that is not likely to be permitted in future).[10]

Source: Biplab Sarkar.

---

[10] A recent central government announcement states that the Food Corporation of India (FCI) will not take on the monetary procurement burden of such States where procurement is organised by announcing a bonus on the centrally announced MSP.

almost all the major items; the gap is particularly large in the case of cost of labour, machines and, for cotton, plant protection chemicals.

One factor responsible for variation in incomes across classes was differences in cropping pattern. Landlords and big capitalist farmers cultivated sugarcane and other high-value crops on part of their holdings, which were sold at high prices in sugar mills/markets that were somewhat far and not easily accessible to other farmers.

Another feature of note is that the costs of machine labour exceeded the costs of human labour in the cultivation of all crops. As discussed below, this reflects the high level of mechanisation of agriculture in Gulabewala village.

USE OF MACHINES IN AGRICULTURE

A notable feature of the agrarian economy of 25 F Gulabewala is the extensive use of machines in agriculture. The first reaper, a local innovation by a leading farmer of the village, was deployed in agriculture in the 1960s. In 2007–08, ploughing was almost entirely done by tractors. Machines were deployed on a large scale for weeding and for spraying plant protection chemicals. Harvesting of wheat was done using combine harvesters, following which straw reapers were deployed to harvest the straw.

Table 2.30 shows that the average value of agricultural machinery owned by the Landlords and/or big capitalist farmers 1 group was over Rs 8 lakhs per

Table 2.30 *Average value of machines of different types owned by a household, by class, 25 F Gulabewala* (Rs)

Socio-economic class	Tractors and accessories	Irrigation equipment	Machines for harvesting and post-harvest operations	Other machines	Total
Landlords and/or big capitalist farmers 1	597414	91607	89143	25850	804014
Landlords and/or big capitalist farmers 2	264215	50205	26280	5727	346427
Farmers 1	192371	38009	29312	2481	262173
Farmers 2	55954	0	10735	375	67064

Source: Survey data.

BOX 3: A Note on Ownership and Use of Machines

Agricultural operations in 25 F Gulabewala village were highly mechanised. The value of agricultural machinery and equipment owned per landed household was Rs 2,09,272 in 2007. By way of comparison, according to the All India Debt and Investment Survey (NSSO 2005), in 2002, the value of agricultural machinery per household in Rajasthan was only Rs 7,045. The village survey showed that resident households owned 74 tractors, 53 pump sets, 3 combine harvesters and 11 threshers in the reference year, i.e. 2006–07.

The ownership of machines, however, was highly unequal across households: big farmers (owning more than 10 hectares each), who comprised 18.5 per cent of all households, owned between them 56 tractors, 42 pump sets, 3 harvesters and 10 threshers (Table 1).[11] The Gini coefficient of the value of agricultural machinery and equipment was 0.84 (as compared to a Gini coefficient of 0.81 for land ownership; see Table 2). In other words, ownership of agricultural machinery was more unequal than ownership of land.

Table 1 *Distribution of number and share of agricultural machinery by size class of operational holding, 25 F Gulabewala, 2007*

Land size (hectare)	Tractor		Pump set		Harvester		Thresher	
	Number	% of total	Number	% of total	Number	% of total	Number	% of total
Landless	0	0	1	2	0	0	0	0
0.1–2	0	0	1	2	0	0	0	0
2.01–4	7	9	1	2	0	0	0	0
4.01–10	11	15	8	15	0	0	1	9
>10	56	76	42	79	3	100	10	91
Total	74	100	53	100	3	100	11	100

Source: Survey data.

While the ownership of machinery was highly unequal, the use of machines was less so. For example, while 45 per cent of households owned pump sets, 66 per cent of households reported using pump sets for irrigation (Table 3). Similarly, only 17 per cent of households owned threshers, but threshers were used by 93 per cent of households.

[11] This definition of big farmer is based totally on land ownership.

Table 2 *Gini coefficient of productive assets related to agriculture and allied activities, 25 F Gulabewala, 2007*

Type of asset	Gini
Agricultural land	0.81
Agricultural machinery	0.84
Land preparation	0.85
Irrigation equipment	0.86
Harvest and post- harvest equipment	0.95
Animal resources	0.78

Source: Survey data.

Table 3 *Proportion of households owning and using selected machines across different size-classes of operational holding, 25 F Gulabewala, 2006–07*

Land size (hectare)	Tractor		Pump set		Thresher	
	Owning	Using	Owning	Using	Owning	Using
>0–4	43.7	81.2	6.2	25	0	75
4.01–10	81.8	100	54.5	72.7	9.1	100
> 10	92.1	100	57.9	81.6	26.3	100
All	78.5	95.4	44.6	66.1	16.9	93.8

Source: Survey data.

Most agricultural operations were done with machines. In the case of cotton, ploughing was entirely by tractors, 90 per cent of sowing was by tractors with a seed-drill, and two-thirds of irrigation was by machines. In the case of wheat, all the ploughing and sowing were done with tractors, and all threshing was with combine harvesters or threshers.

Not surprisingly, smaller landowners depended more on rented machines than larger landowners. This is clear from the data on cotton cultivation and wheat cultivation. Only 5 per cent of ploughing for cotton was with hired machines in the case of landowners operating more than 10 hectares. By contrast, 36 per cent of ploughing was undertaken with hired tractors by those operating less than 10 hectares.

Similarly, in the case of wheat, 38 per cent of sowing was done with hired machines by those operating less than 10 hectares, while those with more than 10 hectares hardly hired machines for sowing.

> To conclude, all major crop operations in Gulabewala village were mechanised. The bigger farmers owned machines whereas the smaller farmers hired machines for use.
>
> *Source*: Anupam Sarkar (2013).

Table 2.31 *Proportion of households that owned different types of machines, by class, 25 F Gulabewala* (per cent)

Socio-economic class	Tractors and accessories	Irrigation equipment	Machines for harvesting and post-harvest operations	Other machines
Landlords and/or big capitalist farmers 1	100	100	100	100
Landlords and/or big capitalist farmers 2	100	85	38	92
Farmers 1	100	69	31	100
Farmers 2	58	0	42	92

Source: Survey data.

household. Tractors and accessories used for land preparation and weeding were the most important component of capital stock in agriculture. Table 2.31 shows that all Landlord and/or big capitalist farmer households, as well as all Farmer 1 households, owned tractors.

As Box 3 shows, while ownership of agricultural machinery was highly concentrated, its use was widespread.

HOUSEHOLD INCOMES: LEVEL AND DISTRIBUTION

Estimation of household incomes in rural India is difficult given the informal nature of the economy and multiple sources of income – including incomes from self-employment and incomes in kind. The PARI surveys collected data on the following sources of income: crop production; animal resources; wage labour (casual labour in agriculture, long-term labour in agriculture and allied activities, non-agricultural casual employment and long-term employment in non-agricultural activities); salaried jobs; business and trade; moneylending;

pensions and scholarships; remittances and gifts; rental income (from agricultural land, from machinery and from other assets); artisanal work and work at traditional caste calling; and any other source. Using the accounting approach, information from all these sources was used to build an estimate of household income (for the detailed methodology, see FAS 2015).

In 2006–07, at current prices, the mean per capita household income in Gulabewala village was Rs 28,512. The median income, however, was as low at Rs 7,759. We do not have national estimates of household incomes, but the per capita State domestic product (SDP) for Rajasthan the same year was Rs 24,055 at current prices. Based on per capita household income, we estimate that 61 per cent of households in Gulabewala village obtained less than the equivalent of 2 dollars a day (Rs 33 per day).[12] Thus, while the average household income in Gulabewala was higher than the per capita SDP, the distribution was highly unequal with the majority obtaining low incomes (less than 2 dollars a day).

Income levels varied hugely across social groups. The mean per capita income of a Dalit person was Rs 5,531 whereas the mean per capita income of a non-Dalit (mainly Jat Sikh in this case) was Rs 63,408. The ratio of income of a Jat

Table 2.32 *Share of different classes in total household income and mean household income, by socio-economic class, 25 F Gulabewala, 2006–07 (*per cent and Rs)

Socio-economic class	House-holds	Share in total household income (%)	Mean household income (Rs)
Landlords and/or big capitalist farmers 1	3	43	2076014
Landlords and/or big capitalist farmers 2	6	15	391419
Farmers 1	13	20	256297
Farmers 2	6	4	112008
Manual workers	56	9	26059
Business activity/self-employed	6	2	61016
Salaried person/s	5	3	112142
Receives rents, remittances, pensions, handouts	5	3	97751
Total	100	100	163874

Source: Survey data.

[12] This is a conversion from dollars to rupees using purchasing power parity and not the exchange rate.

Sikh person to a Dalit was 11 on average. Box 4 brings out the difference in distribution of incomes across social groups.

Inequality in incomes is even higher when we examine the distribution of incomes across socio-economic classes. Table 2.32 shows the mean income of a household in each class, as well as the share of total village income (or income of all residents) accruing to each socio-economic category. Households in the village belonging to the Landlords and/or big capitalist farmers 1 category accounted for 3 per cent of households and 43 per cent of total household income. Their average income was over Rs 20 lakhs per annum. The top three cultivator classes together accounted for 22 per cent of all households and 78 per cent of total household incomes. By contrast, Manual worker households comprised 56 per cent of all households and received 9 per cent of total household incomes. The average annual income of a Manual worker household was

BOX 4: Caste and Income Distribution

The difference in incomes across social groups is not only in terms of the average. When the distribution of incomes of all Dalit households and Other households was examined, we found that there was a clear non-overlapping of the two frequency distributions (Table 1). All Dalit households reported per capita incomes of less than Rs 20,000 per annum, whereas 68.9 per cent of Other households reported incomes above Rs 20,000 a year.

Table 1 *Distribution of households by annual per capita income and social group, 25 F Gulabewala, 2006–07*

Per capita income (Rs per annum)	Dalits	Others
Less than 5500	63.4	3.7
5500–10000	28.5	6.2
10000–20000	8.1	22.2
20000–30000	0	16.0
30000–40000	0	9.9
40000–50000	0	11.1
Above 50000	0	30.0
All	100	100

Source: Rawal and Swaminathan (2011), Table 13, p. 124.

Table 2.33 *Share of different sources in total household income, by socio-economic class, 25 F Gulabewala, 2006–07 (per cent)*

Socio-economic class	Crop pro-duction	Agri-cultural labour	Rental income from agricultural land	Non-agricultural labour	Salaries	Business and trade	Pensions and remittances	Other sources
Landlords and/or big capitalist farmers 1	57				2	2		39
Landlords and/or big capitalist farmers 2	86		3		8			2
Farmers 1	91		1		3			5
Farmers 2	73	1	5		2	3	10	5
Manual workers	10	65		16	3	1	4	
Business activity/self-employed	6	3	2	7	5	64	7	5
Salaried person/s	6	1	2	1	81		5	5
Receives rents, remittances, pensions, handouts	11		67	1	4		11	6
All households	61	6	3	2	6	3	1	19

Source: Survey data.

Rs 26,059. To put it differently, the per capita household income, on average, of a person from the Landlords and/or big capitalist farmers 1 class was 80 times that of a person from a Manual worker household.

We next turn to the composition of household incomes. Our data show that Gulabewala village was principally an agricultural village: 70 per cent of aggregate household incomes came from the primary sector, 12 per cent from the secondary sector and 18 per cent from the tertiary sector. Further, 93 per cent of households reported some income from the agricultural sector. If we further disaggregate the incomes from the primary sector, 77 per cent came from crop production and only 10 per cent from agricultural wages.

Table 2.33 shows the contribution of different sources of income to total household income across classes. As expected, all categories of landlords and farmers derived the bulk of their income from crop production. However, while income from crop production was 91 per cent of total incomes for Farmers 1 households, it was only 57 per cent of aggregate income for Landlords and/or big capitalist farmers 1 households. The latter had substantial incomes from other sources including moneylending, rental income from buildings and machinery, from shops in the *mandi* (agricultural market), from a dealership for a mobile phone company, from dairying and from salaried jobs. For Manual worker households, 65 per cent of income came from agricultural labour and another 16 per cent from non-agricultural labour.

RURAL MANUAL WORKERS: EMPLOYMENT AND WAGES

This section deals with Manual worker households in the study village, that is, households for whom the major share of income came from manual work. In 25 F Gulabewala, Manual workers was the single largest class of households: 114 households or 56 per cent of all households earned the major share of their incomes from wage employment. Remarkably, there were on average three workers in each Manual worker household.

Turning to the caste composition of this class, we examined:

1. The number of Manual worker households in each caste as a proportion of all Manual worker households;

2. For each caste, the number of Manual worker households in the caste as a proportion of all households in the caste; and

3. The ratio of (1) to (2) or the proportional representation of each caste in the class of Manual workers. A ratio of 1 occurs when the representation of

a particular caste in the said class is exactly proportional to their representation in the population.

The number of Dalit Manual worker households as a proportion of all Manual worker households was as high as 97 per cent in 25 F Gulabewala (indicator 1). At the same time, the proportion of Dalit households belonging to the class of Manual workers was as high as 91 per cent (indicator 2). Not surprisingly, the ratio of indicator 1 to 2 was greater than 1. There was almost perfect overlap between caste (the Dalits) and class (the Manual workers). By contrast, no Jat Sikh (or OBC) household was characterised as a Manual worker household.

Turning to days of employment among members of Manual worker households, on average, a male worker received 141 days of wage employment and a female worker received 67 days of wage employment in the reference year (98 days for all persons). While the average employment for a male worker was a little over six months, further disaggregation showed that 63 per cent of workers received less than three months of wage employment in a year, and only 15 per cent received employment for more than six months (Table 2.34). The distribution of number of days of employment clearly points to pervasive underemployment among rural workers belonging to the class of Manual workers, and raises questions about the reliance of policy-makers on a simple mean or average. To put it another way, 86 per cent of all Manual workers received employment for less than six months in a year.

In most of the PARI surveys, a 'pure agricultural worker household' was non-

Table 2.34 *Distribution of Manual workers, by size-class of number of days of employment, 25 F Gulabewala, 2006–07* (number and per cent)

No. of days of employment	No. of workers	As % of all workers
1 to 30 days	40	16
31 to 60 days	70	28
61 to 90 days	49	19
91 to 120 days	25	10
121 to 150 days	17	7
151 to 180 days	15	6
More than 180 days	38	15
All workers	254	100

Source: Survey data.

existent as all households gained incomes from multiple sources. Further, a 'pure agricultural worker' was also rare, as most Manual workers engaged in both agricultural and non-agricultural employment. In Gulabewala, however, agricultural wage work was the main source of employment for men and women workers.

Table 2.35 shows that 68 per cent of male casual workers and 92 per cent of women casual workers from the Manual worker class in 25 F Gulabewala worked only in agricutural occupations. In terms of days of employment, on average, a male casual worker worked 117 days in agriculture and only 24 days in non-agricultural occupations. A woman casual worker, on average, worked 51 days in agriculture and 16 days in non-agricultural occupations.

Non-agricultural work was scarce in the village. It was scarce for both men and women, but, as in most other villages, it was particularly scarce for women. The main source of non-agricultural employment in Gulabewala was domestic work (for women), and construction and related activities (for men). The ratio between the number of days of agricultural and non-agricultural work in the annual work calendar of a male worker was 117:24. The corresponding figure for a woman worker was 51:16.

Cotton, rapeseed and wheat were the main crops grown. While employment was concentrated in these crops (Table 2.37), widespread mechanisation of wheat

Table 2.35 *Proportion of casual workers in agricultural and non-agricultural occupations, Manual worker class, 25 F Gulabewala, 2006–07* (per cent and days)

Activity	Male	Female	All
Agriculture only	68	92	82
Non-agricultural occupations only	8	3	6
Both agriculture and non-agricultural occupations	23	5	13

Source: Survey data.

Table 2.36 *Average number of days of wage employment obtained by Manual workers in agricultural and non-agricultural work, by sex, 25 F Gulabewala, 2006–07* (8-hour days)

Sex	Agricultural work	Non-agricultural work
Male workers	117	24
Female workers	51	16
All workers	79	19

Source: Survey data.

cultivation restricted manual employment in specific operations (see Box 3).

Daily wages in agricultural operations for male workers ranged from Rs 50 to 100, and they were given food: two meals and tea. For female workers, the daily wages ranged from Rs 40 to 50, and they were given one meal and tea.

Of the 114 households in the Manual worker class, in 50 households, one or more than one member of the household worked as a long-term worker in agricultural and allied activities. In 2007, there were 74 long-term workers (63 men and 11 women) in the village. Female workers were employed on fixed wages. Of all the male workers, six were employed on a share-wage basis and the rest were employed on fixed annual wage contracts. The fixed contracts were mainly for ten to twelve months in a year. Under share-wage contracts, workers and their families who worked on the employer's land received one-fourth of the produce. However, all wage payments for labour used on specific crop operations were paid out of the long-term workers' share. The main activities of long-term male workers were performing agricultural tasks, operating machines, and tending the employer's animals. Female workers performed the tasks of cleaning house premises and cattle-sheds.

A significant section of Dalit long-term worker households did not own their homesteads and huts. These households lived in buildings abandoned by

Table 2.37 *Average number of days of agricultural employment per worker, by crop and sex, 25 F Gulabewala, 2006–07*

Crop	Female workers		Male workers		All workers	
	Days of employment	As % of column	Days of employment	As % of column	Days of employment	As % of column
Cluster bean	0	0	2	2	1	1
Cotton	33	64	63	52	46	56
Fodder crop	0	0	0	0	0	0
Miscellaneous	0	1	1	0	0	1
Oranges	0	0	2	1	1	1
Pulses	1	2	2	2	2	2
Rapeseed	7	13	21	17	13	16
Wheat	10	19	30	25	18	23
All crops	52	100	122	100	81	100

Source: Survey data.

Jat Sikh households who were their landlord–employers. These Dalit workers and their households were engaged in unfree labour relations: on account of their dependence on landlords for shelter, they received lower wages and worked longer hours than workers who owned their houses.

The restricted occupational mobility of Manual workers, particularly Dalit Manual workers, in Gulabewala village is brought out in Box 5.

BOX 5: Intergenerational Occupational Mobility

To what extent do sons remain in the same occupation as their fathers? In this note, we answer this question for all adult males residing in 25 F Gulabewala village. We use a four-fold classification of rural occupations: (1) big/rich farmers; (2) small/poor farmers; (3) skilled workers / salaried persons / persons engaged in business (henceforth skilled workers); and (4) rural manual workers. The categorisation of farmers into big/rich and small/poor is based on the extent of land ownership: those with 20 acres or more are categorised as big farmers. Note that this classification is not the same as that of socio-economic classes in the rest of this chapter.

The method used is of matrix-based mobility tables wherein the diagonal cells represent immobility across successive generations. A simple measure of aggregate mobility, the absolute mobility rate, is the proportion of individuals who fall in the off-diagonal cells of a mobility table.[13]

We first undertook this exercise for all male heads of households and their fathers (see Table 1). We see that 76 per cent of big farmers' sons remained in the same occupation as their fathers and 94 per cent of rural manual workers' sons remained in the same occupation as their fathers. This indicates an almost perfect transmission of advantage and disadvantage from one generation to the next among big/rich farmers and rural manual workers. Not surprisingly, the aggregate mobility rate was as low as 13 per cent (range from 0 to 100 per cent).

We repeated the same exercise for all male heads of households and their *co-resident* adult sons (Table 2). Again, we observe high immobility at both ends of the occupational structure, with 91 per cent of sons of rich farmers remaining in the same occupation and 90 per cent of sons of manual workers remaining in the same occupation. The absolute mobility rate was 16 per cent among this group of males.

---

[13] For further details of the methodology, see Reddy and Swaminathan (2014).

Table 1 *Mobility matrix for male head of household-father pairs by occupation of origin and destination, 25 F Gulabewala, 2006–7*

Fathers' occupation	Sons' occupation				
	Big Farmers	Small Farmers	Skilled workers	Rural manual workers	Total
Big farmers	47	12	3	0	62
	(76)	(19)	(5)	(0)	
Small farmers	1	5	0	6	12
	(8)	(42)	(0)	(50)	
Skilled workers & business	0	1	8	2	11
	0	(9)	(73)	(18)	
Rural manual workers	0	0	7	108	115
	0	0	(6)	(94)	100
Total	48	18	18	116	200
	24	9	9	58	100

Note: Figures in parentheses represent cell values as a percentage of the row
          total.
Source: Survey data.

Table 2 *Mobility matrix for head of household and co-resident son pairs by occupation of origin and destination, 25 F Gulabewala, 2006–7*

Fathers' occupation	Sons' occupation				
	Big farmers	Small farmers	Skilled workers	Rural manual workers	Total
Big farmers	31	0	3	0	34
	(91)	(0)	(9)	(0)	
Small farmers	0	14	2	1	17
	(0)	(82)	(12)	(6)	
Skilled workers	0	1	2	3	6
	(0)	(17)	(33)	(50)	
Rural manual workers	0	0	8	72	80
	(0)	(0)	(10)	(90)	
Total	31	15	15	76	137
	(23)	(11)	(11)	(55)	

Note: Figures in parentheses represent cell values as a percentage of the row total.
Source: Survey data.

We also examined occupational mobility separately for two social groups: Scheduled Castes and all Others (Jat Sikhs in this case). The absolute mobility rate among Scheduled Caste men was lower (10 per cent) than among Jat Sikh men (19 per cent). Notably, there was no Scheduled Caste male in either generation in the category of big farmers. There were seven small farmers among Scheduled Caste 'fathers', but only one son remained a small farmer while the remaining six became rural manual workers.

Rural manual work can be viewed as an occupation of last resort, and so a shift to any other occupation can be treated as upward mobility. Similarly, a shift from any other occupation to rural manual work can be treated as downward mobility. To compare the relative chances of upward and downward mobility among Scheduled Caste men and Jat Sikh men, we use odds ratios. The odds ratio of upward mobility was greater than 1, implying that sons of rural manual workers belonging to non-Dalit social groups had a higher chance of upward mobility than sons of rural manual workers belonging to Scheduled Castes. Specifically, the odds ratio was 2.5, that is, the chances of upward mobility for sons of rural manual workers were 2.5 times higher among Jat Sikh men than among Scheduled Caste men. At the same time, the odds ratios for downward mobility from any occupation to that of rural manual worker was above 1 and very high. Specifically, the odds ratio was 90, implying that the chance of downward mobility among Scheduled Caste men was 90 times that among Jat Sikh men.

Finally, we also examined absolute intergenerational occupational mobility rates over three generations by using matrix-based partial father–son mobility tables, categorised by grandfathers' occupation (Table 3). These data refer to heads of households, their fathers and co-resident sons. The multigenerational mobility matrix indicates a high degree of immobility over three generations at both ends of the occupational structure, i.e. rural manual workers and big farmers. Immobility was most pronounced in the category of rural manual workers. In this village, 91 per cent of men whose grandfathers and fathers were big farmers became big farmers themselves. Similarly, 92 per cent of men whose grandfathers and fathers worked as rural manual workers entered the same occupation. In summary, if we examine the marginal occupational distribution of sons by fathers' (heads of households') occupation for each occupation of the grandfather, men with advantaged grandfathers were more likely to have advantaged fathers and men with disadvantaged grandfathers were more likely to have disadvantaged fathers.

Table 3 *Men's outflow mobility rates by grandfathers' (GF) and father's (F) occupation, 25 F Gulabewala, 2006–07*

		Big farmer (BF)	Small farmer (SF)	Skilled worker (SW)	Rural manual worker (RMW)
GF:BF	F:BF	91	0	9	0
	F:SF	0	80	20	0
	F:SW	0	0	0	0
	F:RMW	0	0	0	0
GF:SF	F:BF	100*	0	0	0
	F:SF	0	86	0	14
	F:SW	0	0	0	0
	F:RMW	0	0	0	0
GF:SW	F:BF	0	0	0	0
	F:SF	0	0	0	0
	F:SW	0	100*	0	0
	F:RMW	0	0	0	0
GF:RMW	F:BF	0	0	0	0
	F:SF	0	0	0	0
	F:SW	0	0	33	67
	F:RMW	0	0	8	92

Note: * The absolute numbers in these cells are very small.
Source: Survey data.

In 25 F Gulabewala, very low intergenerational mobility perpetuated existing occupational polarisation by social group from one generation to the next. These data strongly support the view that Dalit men who remain in Gulabewala village are unable to move out of rural manual labour.

Source: Reddy and Swaminathan (2014).

RURAL CREDIT

Sri Ganganagar district is a relatively well-banked district in the State of Rajasthan, with above average population per bank branch and bank credit per capita. The ratio of bank credit to gross district domestic product in Sri

Ganganagar was 27 per cent in 2010. The rural areas in the district were also well-banked, showing a lower rural population per bank branch and higher rural credit per capita than the State average.

Incidence and Burden of Debt

In 25 F Gulabewala, a village that belonged to a relatively well-banked region within Rajasthan, about 61 per cent of the total number of households were indebted at the time of the survey (Table 2.38).[14] Households which had assets above the village average reported a lower incidence of debt and a lower burden of debt, measured in terms of the debt to asset ratio, than households with assets above the village average. The debt to asset ratio for households having assets above the village average was 2.2 per cent as against 9.7 per cent for households having assets below the village average.

Table 2.38 *Basic indicators of indebtedness, all households, and below and above average asset-owning households, 25 F Gulabewala, 2006–07*

	All households	Households with assets below average	Households with assets above average
Percentage of indebted households	61.3	74.7	52.0
Average amount of debt (Rs)	77,798	25,017	243,365
Debt–assets ratio (per cent)	4.2	12.5	3.5

Source: Survey data.

Sources of Debt

The share of formal sources in total debt of households in 25 F Gulabewala was about 75 per cent, which was remarkably higher than the State average (as reported in the *All India Debt and Investment Survey*, AIDIS, for 2002). As already noted, the village belonged to a well-banked district in Rajasthan. Banks were thus the most important source of formal credit in the village. The village

[14] Following the definition given in the AIDIS, debt refers to cash debt outstanding as on the date of the survey, irrespective of whether it was paid in cash or kind. The estimates for percentage of indebted households and amount of debt in 25 F Gulabewala were significantly higher than those provided for Rajasthan by the AIDIS of 2002. This point also holds true in the case of Rewasi. Although the years of the village survey and AIDIS are not comparable, this relates to a broader point about the possibility of an underestimation of debt by the AIDIS, which was referred to earlier.

households had access to a commercial bank branch and a cooperative agriculture and rural development bank (earlier termed land development bank).

The share of formal sources in total debt may be influenced by a few large bank loans. To check this, we examined the number of loans and found that only 36 per cent of all loans were taken from formal sources. Informal sources accounted for the remaining 63 per cent of loans taken by residents of the village.

There were a variety of informal lenders operating in the village credit system including traders/commission agents (*aadhti*), employers, landlords, shopkeepers, professional moneylenders, friends and relatives, and self-help groups (SHGs). Professional moneylenders were not important in this village. Traders and commission agents were the most dominant source of informal credit in the village. The agents gave large-sized loans to Jat Sikh cultivators for purchase of inputs. These loans were commonly repaid after harvesting. As the village survey was done in the month of June, most of the loans had been repaid and, as a result, could not be captured in the survey. In part, this has resulted in an underestimation of the share of informal sources in the village credit system.

Table 2.39 *Share in total debt by source, 25 F Gulabewala, 2007*

Village	Amount of debt (Rs)	Share in total debt	Number of loans	Share in total number of loans
Formal sources	*1,18,91,299*	*74.9*	*72*	*36.9*
Commercial banks	1,08,60,865	68.5	63	32.1
Cooperatives	10,20,987	5.8	8	4.1
Other formal sources	9,447	3.2	1	0.5
Informal sources	*39,79,426*	*25.1*	*124*	*63.1*
Professional moneylenders	52,372	0.3	2	1.0
SHGs/MFIs	42,851	0.3	2	1.0
Employers	50,786	0.3	1	0.5
Landlords	12,58,076	7.9	68	34.9
Small and medium peasants	1,586	0.01	1	0.5
Traders/commission agents/ other service providers	23,27,950	14.7	18	9.1
Other occasional lenders	2,45,805	1.5	32	16.1
Total	*1,58,70,725*	*100.0*	*196*	*100.0*

Source: Survey data.

Another indicator of the dependence on informal sources of credit in the village is the percentage of households borrowing *only* from informal sources during the year as compared to those borrowing *only* from formal sources (Table 2.40). Only 20 per cent of indebted households in the village met their credit needs from only formal sources, whereas 70 per cent of households relied only on informal credit and did not report any loan from formal sources during the survey year.

Table 2.40 *Percentage of households borrowing only from formal/ informal sources and both sources during the survey year, 25 F Gulabewala, 2006–07* (per cent)

Source	%
Only from formal sources	20
Only from informal sources	70
From both sources	9
From any source	100

Source: Survey data.

Table 2.41 *Share of formal and informal sources in total number of loans, caste-wise, 25 F Gulabewala, 2007* (per cent)

Source	Dalit	Jat Sikhs	All
Formal sources	*19.0*	*66.2*	*36.9*
Commercial banks	17.1	56.9	31.8
Cooperatives	0.95	7.7	3.5
Other formal sources	0.95	1.6	1.5
Informal sources	*81.0*	*33.8*	*63.1*
Professional moneylenders	–	3.1	1.0
SHGs/MFIs	1.9	–	1.0
Employers	0.9	–	0.5
Landlords	50.5	4.6	34.9
Small and medium peasants	0.9	–	0.5
Traders/commission agents/ other service providers	3.8	16.4	7.7
Other occasional lenders	23.0	9.7	17.6
Total	*100.0*	*100.0*	*100.0*

Source: Survey data.

There is a clear differential in access to formal credit as between Dalit households and Jat Sikh households (Table 2.41). Of all loans taken during the survey year, 81 per cent were from informal lenders among Dalit households. Among Jat Sikh households, 66 per cent of loans were from the formal sector. When disaggregated further, we found that Dalit households borrowed most frequently from landlords, whereas for Jat Sikh households the main source of informal credit was the trader/commission agent.

We now turn to differences across socio-economic classes (Table 2.42). The share of formal sources in total debt outstanding was 91 per cent among Landlords and/or big capitalist farmers 1 households. The corresponding share was 37 per cent for Manual worker households. In terms of the number of loans, only 16 per cent of loans taken by Manual worker households were from the formal sector. Manual worker households had very limited access to formal sources of credit in Gulabewala village.

Within the informal sector too, there was a differential across classes (Table 2.43). Landlords and/or big capitalist farmers 1 households relied almost entirely on traders/commission agents and shopkeepers. Farmer households (both categories, 1 and 2) relied on landlords and capitalist farmers, traders/ commission agents and professional moneylenders. Salaried persons households relied on their employers and shopkeepers. While Manual workers households

Table 2.42 *Share of formal sources in total debt outstanding and number of loans, by socio-economic classes, 25 F Gulabewala, 2007* (per cent)

Socio-economic class	Share of formal sources in	
	Debt outstanding	Number of loans
Landlords and/or big capitalist farmers 1 households	91.3	87.5
Landlords and/or big capitalist farmers 2 households	73.6	63.6
Farmers 1 households	72.6	60.0
Farmers 2 households	95.2	69.6
Manual workers households	36.5	15.7
Households receiving rents, remittances, pensions, handouts	96.2	83.3
Salaried persons households	97.8	66.7
Households engaged in business activity/ self-employed	10.6	10.0
All households	74.9	36.9

Source: Survey data.

Table 2.43 *Share of debt outstanding from informal sources, by type of source and socio-economic class, 25 F Gulabewala, 2006–07 (per cent)*

Informal sources	Socio-economic class number								
	Landlords and/or big capitalist farmers 1 households	Landlords and/or big capitalist farmers 2 households	Farmers 1 households	Farmers 2 households	Manual worker households	Households receiving rents, remittances, pensions, handouts	Salaried persons households	Households engaged in business activity/self-employed	All households
Friends and relatives	–	–	–	–	6.1	–	–	–	1.8
Landlords/capitalist farmers	–	–	23.9	8.3	79.1	–	–	74.3	31.7
Employers	–	–	–	–	0.4	–	83.7	–	0.3
Professional moneylenders	–	–	12.4	–	–	–	–	–	1.3
Salaried persons	–	–	–	–	0.4	–	–	–	0.1
Self-help groups	–	–	–	–	0.4	–	–	–	0.1
Shop loans	–	2.0	–	8.3	1.4	100.0	16.3	–	1.8
Trader/other service providers	100.0	98.0	63.7	–	9.1	–	–	–	58.5
Workers	–	–	–	–	0.2	–	–	22.3	1.9
Other unspecified informal sources	–	–	–	83.4	2.9	–	–	3.4	2.4
All informal sources	100.0	100.0	100.0	100.0	100.0	100.0	100.0	100.0	100.0

Note: For details about class categories, see Table 2.5.
Source: Survey data.

borrowed from all major types of informal sources, the capitalist farmer was the most important lender for them.

Interest Rates on Debt

About 68 per cent of the total debt was contracted at interest rates ranging between 0 and 20 per cent: rates generally charged by formal agencies (Table 2.44). However, in terms of the number of loans, only 37 per cent of the total loans were taken at interest rates below 20 per cent. Even with a relatively well-developed banking infrastructure, about one-fourth of the total loans in the village carried rates between 30 and 40 per cent per annum. In the informal sector zero-interest loans from friends and relatives accounted for another 23 per cent of total loans.

The weighted average rate of interest in 25 F Gulabewala was about 13 per cent, but the modal rate of interest was 24 per cent (Table 2.45). Mean and modal interest rates by source of debt are shown in Table 2.46.

In Table 2.47, we show the burden of debt using two indicators: the ratio of total debt to total assets, and the ratio of annual interest payment to ratio of assets. The striking feature of our calculation is that debt outstanding accounts for more than half the value of total assets owned by Manual worker households and the interest payment alone accounts for 21 per cent of total assets. The burden of debt falls heavily on Manual worker households in Gulabewala.

Table 2.44 *Distribution of amount of debt and number of loans by interest rates, 25 F Gulabewala, 2007*

Rate of interest	Amount of debt (Rs)	Share in amount of debt (per cent)	Number of loans	Share in number of loans (per cent)
0	4,19,900	2.6	44	22.5
0 < rate < 15	41,77,995	26.3	23	11.7
15 < rate < 20	66,54,604	42.0	50	25.5
20 < rate < 30	21,48,422	13.5	16	8.2
30 < rate < 40	18,65,254	11.8	53	27.0
40 < rate < 50	2,04,550	1.3	8	4.1
Unspecified	4,00,000	2.5	2	1.0
Total	*1,58,70,725*	*100.0*	*196*	*100.0*

Source: Survey data.

Table 2.45 *Weighted average/ modal and range of rates of interest, 25 F Gulabewala, 2007* (per cent)

Weighted average interest rate	Modal rate of interest	Range of interest rate (min–max)
13.1	24	0–36

Notes: 1. Weights are defined as the share of debt taken at each interest rate in total debt.
2. These calculations exclude usufruct loans and loans involving land and credit linkages.
Source: Survey data.

Table 2.46 *Mean and modal rates of interest by informal source, 25 F Gulabewala, 2007* (per cent, per annum)

Source category	Mean	Mode
Friends and relatives	0	0
Employers	12	–
Landlords/capitalist farmers	14	0
Professional moneylenders	18	18
Self-help groups	12	12
Shop loans	21	18
Trader/Commission agents/other service providers	21	24
Workers	24	24
Salaried persons	24	24
Other and unspecified informal sources	20	0

Source: Survey data.

Table 2.47 *Debt and interest outstanding to assets ratio, by socio-economic class, 25 F Gulabewala* (per cent)

Socio-economic class	Debt–Asset ratio	Interest outstanding to asset ratio
Landlords and/or big capitalist farmers 1 households	2.2	0.1
Landlords and/or big capitalist farmers 2 households	7.2	1.1
Farmers 1 households	2.0	0.1
Farmers 2 households	5.8	1.2
Manual workers households	52.6	20.8
All classes	4.2	0.7

Source: Survey data.

Purposes of Debt

Formal sources largely supported activities that were directly income-generating, including agriculture and allied activities, and non-farm production activities. About 58 per cent of the total debt taken from formal sources was for such activities (Table 2.48). However, of the total debt owed to the formal sector, about 42 per cent was for financing consumption. Informal sources were, of course, more used for activities that were not directly income-generating (86 per cent; see Table 2.49).

Table 2.48 *Distribution of amount of debt by purpose, 25 F Gulabewala, 2007*

Purpose	Amount of debt (Rs)	Share in amount of debt (per cent)
Directly income-generating	*74,02,606*	*46.60*
Agriculture	37,69,523	23.80
Non-agriculture	36,33,083	22.90
Not directly income-generating	*84,68,119*	*53.40*
Ceremonial expenditure	16,84,199	10.60
Housing	14,09,680	8.90
Medical expenses	7,26,535	4.60
Education	3,450	0.02
All other household expenses	48,44,255	30.50
Total	1,58,70,725	100.00

Source: Survey data.

Table 2.49 *Share of debt taken from formal and informal sources for various purposes, 25 F Gulabewala, 2007 (per cent)*

	Debt taken from formal sources for	Debt taken from informal sources for
Directly income-generating activities	58	14
Activities that are not directly income-generating	42	86
Total	100	100

Source: Survey data.

ACCESS TO BASIC AMENITIES

Economic and social disparities in 25 F Gulabewala are also reflected in access to basic amenities.

The Census of India defines a *pucca* house as one with roof and walls made of *pucca* or permanent materials. Table 2.50 shows that 79 per cent of Jat Sikh households in Gulabewala had houses with *pucca* roofs, walls and floors, while only 3 per cent of Dalit households had houses with *pucca* roofs, walls and floors. A very large majority of Jat Sikh households, 98 per cent, had houses with more than one room, while 26 per cent of Dalit households lived in single-room structures. A striking feature of the central settlement of 25 F Gulabewala, where the Jat Sikhs lived, was that the houses had large courtyards that were used to store machinery as well as to stock cotton bushes that were used as fuel. In contrast, the two settlements where Mazhabi Sikhs and Nayaks lived had small houses with few open spaces. The difference in availability of space is clear from the following statistic: the total area of homestead land of all Dalit households in the village was 189,394 square feet, whereas the area of the two largest homesteads among Jat Sikh households was 210,362 square feet.

Disparities in access to basic amenities are clearly seen in Table 2.51. While 99 per cent of Jat Sikh households had electricity in their houses, the corresponding proportion was only 65 per cent for Dalit households. Similarly, 99 per cent of Jat Sikh households had toilets in their houses whereas only 77 per cent of Dalit households had toilets. About 97 per cent of Jat Sikh houses had

Table 2.50 *Proportion of households having* pucca *houses and proportion of households having only a single room in the house, by social group and socio-economic class, 25 F Gulabewala, 2007* (per cent)

Social group and socio-economic class	Houses with *pucca* roof, walls and floor	Single-room houses
Social group		
Jat Sikhs	79	2
Dalits	3	26
Socio-economic class		
Landlords and farmers	79	0
Manual workers	3	30
All households	32	18

Source: Survey data.

Table 2.51 *Proportion of houses with electricity connections, toilets and a source of water within the homestead, by social group, 25 F Gulabewala, 2007* (per cent)

Social group	Houses with electricity	Houses with toilets	Houses with a source of water
Jat Sikhs	99	99	97
Dalits	65	77	48
All	77	85	67

Source: Survey data.

a source of water supply within their homestead; the corresponding proportion for Dalits was 48 per cent.

The right to adequate housing is recognised as a basic human right by the United Nations and its constituent bodies. We attempted a simple computation from our village data: we listed a series of criteria which, although they fell far short of the criteria listed by the United Nations or the International Labour Organisation, represented a basic measure of the quality of housing in India. The criteria we listed for a house were: (1) *pucca* roofs, walls and floors; (2) two rooms; (3) a source of water inside or immediately outside the house; (4) an electricity connection (authorised or unauthorised); and (5) a functioning latrine (Singh, Swaminathan and Ramachandran 2014).

In 25 F Gulabewala village, in aggregate, 32 per cent of households lived in houses that met all five criteria. Disaggregated by social group, a staggering 97 per cent of Dalit households lived in houses which did not meet our criteria of adequate housing. The corresponding proportion was 24 per cent among Jat Sikhs and other OBC households.

If the same definition is used, data for different socio-economic classes (in Table 2.52) show that only one Manual worker household lived in a house which met all the specified conditions, and 109 households (99 per cent of Manual worker households) lived in houses where at least one criterion was not met.

In rural India, most households own their dwelling place, even if it is only a mud-and-thatch hut. According to the Census of India 2011, 95 per cent of all households and 96 per cent of Dalit households owned their dwelling place. A distinct feature of Gulabewala village was that 20 per cent of Dalit households *did not own* their dwelling place. The majority of these households lived in accommodation provided by their landlord-employers. A detailed study by Shamsher Singh (2014) showed that 19 such Dalit Manual worker households

Table 2.52 *Number and percentage of households (HHs) with fully* pucca *house (roof, walls and floor made of* pucca *materials), electricity connection, 2 rooms, toilet, water within or in front of house, by socio-economic class, 25 F Gulabewala*

Socio-economic class	With all 5		Not with all 5		Total
	HHs	%	HHs	%	HHs
Landlords and/or big capitalist farmers 1/2, Farmers 1/2	44	79	12	21	56
Manual workers	1	1	109	99	110
All	58	30	138	70	196

Source: Survey data.

lived in very poor conditions of housing, in structures usually abandoned by their Jat Sikh employers and adjacent to the employer's cattle-shed. Most of these structures were fully *katcha* – that is, the walls, floor and roof were made of *katcha* or temporary materials – and had no electricity. However, most had *katcha* latrines: 'simple pits and not sanitary toilets' that would be classified as 'unimproved sanitation by the United Nations' (Singh 2014, p. 201). These toilets were constructed because of social pressure from the Jat Sikh employers, who did not want the workers to defecate on their cotton fields.

Further, through detailed case studies, Singh shows that provision of housing, even though of very low quality, was linked to labour relations between the Dalit Manual workers and the Jat Sikh landlord-employers. When workers were provided a small plot of land on which to build a hut or an abandoned structure, they either worked for lower wages or extra hours, or members of their family worked free for the landlord. In other words, because of their dependence on their employer for a simple hut, Dalit households were often trapped in unfree labour relations. And, even after several years of employment, Dalit Manual worker households were unable to make even basic improvements to their houses without the permission of their landlord-employers.

The data and analysis presented in this chapter show clear signs of the development of capitalist agriculture in 25 F Gulabewala village of Sri Ganganagar district, Rajasthan. Crop production in Gulabewala is characterised by high yields and income, high levels of mechanisation, and low levels of use of family labour. Differentiation has led to the emergence of two major classes in the village: capitalist farmers and rural manual workers. This differentiation is associated with a high degree of landlessness, high inequality in the ownership of land and other assets, and, consequently, very high inequality in incomes.

A distinctive feature of the village is the near-perfect correlation between class and caste. Dalit households – from both Sikh and Hindu backgrounds – comprised the landless, asset-less rural proletariat. The Jat Sikh households (classified as Other Backward Classes or OBC in Rajasthan) were landowning capitalist farmers.

Gulabewala village is a classic example of the paradox of the Indian countryside, namely, the development of productive forces and capitalist agriculture alongside the persistence of unfree labour relations and discriminatory social relations.

APPENDIX

Appendix Table A1.1 *Assets in each asset category as a proportion of all assets, by selected socio-economic class, 25 F Gulabewala, 2007 (per cent)*

Socio-economic class	Land and water bodies (including trees)	Houses, homestead land, any other land and buildings	Animals and livestock (including draught animals)	Means of production	Means of transport	Domestic durable goods	Other assets (inventories)	All assets
Landlords and/or big capitalist farmers: 1/2, Farmer: 1/2	84	10	0.9	2.8	0.6	0.6	1	100
Manual worker	4.4	78.3	8.8	0.2	0.4	5.7	2.1	100
All households	83.5	11.4	1	2.6	0.7	0.7	1	100

Source: Survey data.

Appendix Table A1.2 *Proportion of different types of assets owned, by selected socio-economic class, 25 F Gulabewala, 2007 (per cent)*

Socio-economic class	Land and water bodies (including trees)	Houses, homestead land, any other land and buildings	Animals and livestock (including draught animals)	Means of production	Means of transport	Domestic durable goods	Other assets (inventories)	All assets
Landlords and/or big capitalist farmers:1/2, Farmer:1/2	93	79	86	96.5	84	73	93	91
Manual worker	0.0	6.2	8.2	0.1	0.6	6.9	1.9	0.9
All households	100	100	100	100	100	100	100	100

Note: Column total does not add up to 100 as not all categories are reported.
Source: Survey data.

3

Agrarian Relations in Rewasi

INTRODUCTION TO THE STUDY VILLAGE

Rewasi village in Sikar block of Sikar district is about 31 kilometres from Sikar town on the Sikar–Salasar road. A *pucca* road connects the main habitation of the village with the Sikar–Salasar road. The railway station nearest to Rewasi is at Sikar. The nearest market is in Sewad Badi, 6 kilometres away on the Sikar–Salasar road. There is a health sub-centre in the village which provides only first-aid facilities. For other medical services, people have to travel to the primary health centre in Phagalwa, at a distance of 9 kilometres, or to the block/ district hospital in Sikar which is 31 kilometres away. There is one primary school, one upper primary school and one high school (privately owned) in the village. Students from Rewasi also study in schools in neighbouring villages.

At the time of our survey in 2010, there were 220 households resident in the village. However, as information on one household is incomplete, all the analysis here pertains to 219 households. Rewasi is a multi-caste village. Jats are economically and politically the dominant caste. Jat households, once tenants of Rajput *jagirdar*s, obtained ownership rights over land as a result of the abolition of different forms of statutory landlordism. In contrast, the Rajputs no longer hold the same position of dominance in the village that they once did. There are also Brahman, Meena (Scheduled Tribe) and Meghwal (Dalit) households in Rewasi. Most households in the village own land, although there is substantial inequality in the extent of ownership of land across social groups and classes.

Rewasi village belongs to the Transitional Plain of Inland Drainage (TPID) category of the Western Dry agroclimatic region of Rajasthan. The reference year of the survey, 2009–10, was a year of monsoon failure. As shown in Table

3.1, annual rainfall in Rajasthan in 2009–10 was 28 per cent below normal and 28 districts including Sikar were declared as drought-affected. In Rewasi, the kharif crop was almost completely destroyed as a result of low rainfall during the monsoon. In the semi-arid eastern plain zone of Rajasthan, failure of monsoon rains and kharif crops is not a rare occurrence.

The analysis of the agrarian economy of Rewasi presented here, based on data from the survey of 2009–10, reflects economic conditions in a year of severe climatic stress on account of low rainfall.

Pearl millet is the most important crop of the kharif season in the village. In the rabi season, land irrigated by tubewells is sown with wheat, mustard, onions and fenugreek. In a village characterised by sandy soils and low rainfall,

Table 3.1 *Annual rainfall in Rajasthan (in millimetres and as percentage deviation from normal rainfall), 2006–07 to 2010–11*

Year	Rainfall (mm)	Percentage deviation from normal rainfall (575.1 mm)
2006–07	688.0	19.6
2007–08	513.8	−10.6
2008–09	555.2	−3.5
2009–10	436.6	−23.9
2010–11	696.6	50.3

Source: Department of Agriculture, Government of Rajasthan; http://www.krishi. rajasthan.gov.in/departments/agriculture/pdf/Rainfall_21_02_2014.pdf.

Table 3.2 *Land use, Rewasi, 2001*

Village			Area (in hectares)	As % of geo-graphical area
Geographical area			616.0	100.0
Land use (as % of geographical area)	Forest		0.0	0.0
	Area under cultivation	Irrigated	244.6	39.7
		Unirrigated	275.7	44.8
	Cultivable waste		46.9	7.6
	Area not available for cultivation		48.8	7.9

Source: Census of India, 2001.

access to irrigation is critical, though limited (Table 3.2). There are about 75 tubewells in the village. These irrigate about 40 per cent of the net sown area. Tubewells are used mainly in the rabi season. The kharif crop is mainly rainfed, even where land holdings are in the command area of tubewells. Cultivation on unirrigated land in the kharif season is dependent entirely on rainfall, and the land is not cultivated in the rabi season.

Animal resources – the people tend cattle, camels and goats – are an important source of household incomes in Rewasi. The maintenance of animals depends crucially on fodder from field crops and leaves of the *khejuri* (*Prosopis cineraria*) tree.

Another important aspect of the village economy is the high rate of migration to other cities in India as well as to countries of the Persian Gulf. Remittances from migrants are an important source of income for many households.

Demography

Table 3.3 presents the distribution of the resident village population by age-group and sex. Males outnumber females in the age-group of 0 to 6 years, with the result that the child sex ratio (CSR) is 835 females per 1,000 males. However, females strongly outnumber males in the age-group of 18 to 49 years. This is because a large number of adult males, 135 in all, belonging to families in the village reside outside the village as migrant workers and are not therefore resident members of households of the village. As a result, the population sex ratio (PSR) for the village is 1,183 females per 1,000 males.

The rural CSR for the district of Sikar in 2011 was 836, almost the same as for Rewasi in 2010. The CSR figure for rural Rajasthan was higher, at 886 as per the 2011 Census, itself a steep decline from 914 in 2001. The PSR for rural Rajasthan was 930 in 2001 and rose marginally to 932 in 2011. The rural PSR for the district of Sikar in 2011 was 948. If the 135 non-resident adult males are included as part of the male population of Rewasi, its PSR in 2010 becomes 910, lower than that for rural Sikar as well as rural Rajasthan.

Let us turn now to the size distribution of households in Rewasi (Table 3.4). The average household size in the village was 5.9, somewhat higher than that of Rajasthan, at 5.5.

Table 3.3 *Distribution of population by age and sex, Rewasi, 2010*

Age-group	Population			As % of total population		
	Female	Male	Persons	Female	Male	Persons
0 to <3 years	34	42	76	5.0	6.9	5.9
3 to 6 years	52	61	113	7.6	10.0	8.7
7 to 9 years	46	52	98	6.7	8.6	7.6
10 to 14 years	100	82	182	14.6	13.5	14.1
15 to 17 years	45	51	96	6.6	8.4	7.4
18 to 24 years	78	63	141	11.4	10.4	10.9
25 to 34 years	121	67	188	17.7	11.0	14.6
35 to 49 years	100	85	185	14.6	14.0	14.3
50 to 59 years	43	46	89	6.3	7.6	6.9
60 to 69 years	35	33	68	5.1	5.4	5.3
≥70 years	31	25	56	4.5	4.1	4.3
All	685	607	1292	100.0	100.0	100.0

Source: Survey data.

Table 3.4 *Distribution of households by household size, Rewasi, 2010*

Household size	Number of households	As percentage of all households	Average size of household	Cumulative number of persons	Cumulative percentage of the population
1	2	0.9	1	2	0.2
2	18	8.2	2	38	2.9
3	22	10.0	3	104	8.0
4	40	18.2	4	264	20.4
5	41	18.6	5	469	36.3
6	32	14.5	6	661	51.2
7	22	10.0	7	815	63.1
≥8	43	19.5	11.1	1292	100.0
All	220	100.0	5.9	1292	100.0

Source: Survey data.

Table 3.5 *Number and percentage of households, by social group, Rewasi, 2009–10*

Social group	Number of households	Per cent
Brahman	5	2.2
Rajput	87	39.7
Jat (OBC)	65	29.6
Other OBC	19	8.6
Dalit	21	9.6
Meena (ST)	21	9.6
Unspecified	1	0.4
All	219	100

Source: Survey data.

Social Composition of Households

Of the 219 households living in Rewasi in 2010, 87 were Rajputs, numerically the biggest caste in the village. Sixty-five households belonged to the dominant Jat caste (classified as OBC in Rajasthan). There were five Brahman households in the village. Other OBC castes in Rewasi were Jangid (carpenter), Lohar (blacksmith) and Kumawat (potter). The largest Dalit caste in the village was Meghwal (twenty households), and there was one Mochi (Dalit) household in the village. There were twenty-one Meena (Scheduled Tribe) households in the village.

SOCIO-ECONOMIC CLASSES

Incomes and levels of labour deployment on land in Rewasi tend to fluctuate considerably from year to year. Therefore, using data on incomes and labour deployment for a single year to classify households has its limitations. This problem was amplified in the survey year because it was not a 'normal' year: the survey was conducted in a year in which kharif crops had failed on account of low monsoon rainfall. Nevertheless it is also the case that such crop failures are not infrequent in the semi-arid regions of Rajasthan. With the failure of kharif crops, incomes from crop production plummeted for most households in Rewasi. Also, very little labour was deployed on land since crops were abandoned early. In view of this, the composition of income and pattern of labour deployment in the village in 2009–10 were different from that in a 'normal' year. For this reason, unlike in the other villages, we have not used data on incomes and labour use for the classification of peasant households in Rewasi.

The socio-economic classification of households in Rewasi, using the PARI survey data, was based on the following broad scheme (Tables 3.6 and 3.7).[1] First, eight households that were among the richest in the village and wielded considerable social and political power in the village were identified and classified separately as 'Landlords and rural rich'. It is noteworthy that, in Rewasi, these households did not come from historically dominant landlord families. They came from different caste and economic backgrounds, but had risen economically and in terms of their political position in the village. Jat households in the village had acquired ownership rights over land as a result of *jagirdari* abolition. These households were direct beneficiaries of the Shekhawati peasant movement in the area, which was led by Jats, and had culminated in abolition of Jagirdari rights (see Appendix 1). Jat households in this class had further accumulated land and prospered economically by investing in non-agricultural businesses in the village and in Sikar town. Brahman households were engaged in non-agricultural businesses in the village and had also ac-cumulated large amounts of land. The sole Dalit household in this class was the largest landowning household in the village. The head of this household had been given a large amount of land by the government as a reward for his work in the Indian army.

Households primarily engaged in non-agricultural businesses were identified and classified separately. Of the remaining households, first, households pri-marily dependent on salaried employment, next, households primarily engaged in artisan work, and then, households primarily dependent on pensions and petty hand-outs, were identified and classified separately.

Hired worker households were those whose members worked as wage labourers in agricultural and non-agricultural tasks. Many of these households in Rewasi received substantial remittances from family members who worked as wage labourers in skilled and unskilled occupations outside the village. Such remittances along with earnings from manual labour in the village accounted for the bulk of the income of these households in 2009–10. Although all these households operated some land, their holdings were small and their earnings

[1] See Ramachandran (2011).

from crop production were negative in 2009–10 because of widespread crop failure in the kharif season.

The residual households were constituted of peasants. A further classification of peasants was done on the basis of asset ownership, as follows:[2]

Households having means of production valued at more than Rs 20 lakhs per household were classified as 'Peasants 1'. There were 14 households in this class.

Households with means of production valued between Rs 10 lakhs and 20 lakhs per household were classified as 'Peasants 2'. There were 26 households in this class.

Households with means of production valued between Rs 5 lakhs and 10 lakhs per household were classified as 'Peasants 3'. A total of 59 households belonged to this class.

Households with means of production valued at less than Rs 5 lakhs were classified as 'Peasants 4'. The number of households in this class was 53.

In all, households were classified into ten socio-economic categories (Table 3.6).

Compared to other villages, the correlation between caste and class was not as sharp in Rewasi (Table 3.7). As already mentioned, households from Brahman, Jat and Dalit backgrounds belonged to the class of the rural rich. Rajputs and Jats formed the bulk of the peasantry, though Scheduled Caste and Scheduled Tribe (Meena) households were also peasant households. The majority of Hired worker households were Rajput or Dalit households. It should be noted, however, that Scheduled Castes and Scheduled Tribes were over-represented among the poorer peasants (i.e. Peasants 3 and 4 categories).

The class structure of contemporary Rewasi bears a marked influence of the peasant struggles that took place in the Shekhawati region from the 1920s through the 1940s, and culminated in the abolition of the *jagirdari* system. From the medieval period through the mid-twentieth century, agrarian conditions in Shekhawati were characterised by dominant control of Rajput *jagirdars* over land. This was fundamentally changed as a result of peasant struggles in the first half of the twentieth century, which culminated in abolition of *jagirdari*. While *jagirdars* and Rajput princes in other parts of Rajasthan retained control over large tracts of land, this was not the case in Shekhawati. In Shekhawati, with the abolition of the *jagirdari* system, the dominant control of the Rajputs over land came to an end. Further, given the parasitic nature of the class, the vast

---

[2] As mentioned earlier, we have not used actual income and labour-use for purposes of classification.

Table 3.6 *Number and proportion of households, by socio-economic class, Rewasi, 2009–10*

Socio-economic class	Number	Per cent
Landlords and rural rich	8	3.6
Peasant: 1	14	6.3
Peasant: 2	26	11.8
Peasant: 3	59	26.9
Peasant: 4	53	24.2
Hired workers	39	17.8
Artisan work and work at traditional caste calling	3	1.3
Business activity/self-employed	2	0.9
Salaried person/s	12	5.4
Pensions and handouts	3	1.3
All	219	100.0

Source: Survey data.

Table 3.7 *Distribution of households by social group and socio-economic class, Rewasi, 2009–10*

Socio-economic class	Brahman	Rajput	Jat	Other OBC	Dalit	Meena (ST)	Total
Landlords and rural rich	2	0	5	0	1	0	8
Peasant: 1	0	4	9	1	0	0	14
Peasant: 2	1	12	12	1	0	0	26
Peasant: 3	0	26	16	7	3	7	59
Peasant: 4	1	22	15	3	4	8	53
Hired workers	1	16	4	5	10	3	39
Artisan work and work at traditional caste calling	0	0	0	2	1	0	3
Business activity/ self-employed	0	2	0	0	0	0	2
Salaried person/s	0	3	4	0	2	3	12
Pensions and handouts	0	2	0	0	0	0	2
All	5	87	65	19	21	21	218

Note: One household is excluded from the class of 'Pensions and handouts' as the caste was not reported.
Source: Survey data.

majority of small Rajput *jagirdars* were impoverished as a result of the abolition of *jagirdari*. On the other hand, Jats, an oppressed caste of tenant cultivators who led the peasant struggles, emerged as the dominant caste in Shekhawati. In other words, *jagirdari* abolition in Shekhawati turned upside down the relative positions of Rajput *jagirdars* and Jat tenants in terms of their control over land. In this respect, the effect of legislation on abolition of intermediaries (like *jagirdars* and zamindars) was unique in Shekhawati. (See Appendix 1 on the *jagirdari* system and its abolition.)

LITERACY AND EDUCATION

School Attendance

The data on school attendance and on gross enrolment ratios for Rewasi are presented in Tables 3.8 and 3.9 respectively. School attendance ratios for children between the ages of 6 and 14 years reflect the failure to achieve 100 per cent attendance. Attendance ratios for girls were lower than those for boys in all age-groups. The ratio declined sharply for girls when they completed 14 years of age, which is when they would 'normally' complete eight years of schooling. The ratio for boys declined significantly when they completed 16 years of age, possibly reflecting significant drop-out on completion of Standard X.

Gross enrolment ratios (GER) were lower than attendance rates. While attendance rates averaged 90 per cent among 11 to 14-year-old children, the GER for Standards VI to VIII was significantly lower, around 71 per cent.

Table 3.8 *Number and proportion of children attending school, by age group, by sex, Rewasi, 2010*

Age group	Number of children			As percentage of all children		
	Female	Male	Persons	Female	Male	Persons
6 to 10 years	74	84	158	93.7	96.6	95.2
11 to 14 years	68	65	133	82.9	100.0	90.5
15 to 16 years	25	31	56	64.1	96.9	78.9
17 to 18 years	12	30	42	54.5	75.0	67.7
All	179	210	389	80.6	93.8	87.2

Source: Survey data.

Table 3.9 *Gross enrolment ratio (GER) of children, by level of schooling and sex, Rewasi, 2010*

School level	Number enrolled			GER		
	Female	Male	Persons	Female	Male	Persons
Standard I to V	84	92	176	88.4	90.2	89.3
Standard VI to VIII	50	55	105	61.0	84.6	71.4
Standard IX to X	28	36	64	50.0	80.0	63.4
Standard XI to XII	12	30	42	33.3	58.8	48.3

Note: Gross enrolment ratio (GER) is the total enrolment at a specific level of education, regardless of age, expressed as a percentage of the official school-age population corresponding to the same level of education in a given school year. The Annual Report of the Ministry of Human Resource Development (MoHRD), India, 2008–09 provides data on GER for three levels. The school levels and corresponding school-age for the three levels specified by the MoHRD are as follows: Standards I to V: 6 to 11 years; Standards VI to VIII: 11 to 14 years; and Standards IX to XII: 14 to 18 years. In the Table above, we have divided Standards IX to XII further in two categories: Standards IX to X: 14 to 16 years, and Standards XI to XII: 16 to 18 years.

School attendance and work

We now look at a four-fold classification of children in the age-group of 6 to 18 years: working and attending school; working and not attending school; attending school and not working; not attending school and not working. The data for Rewasi in this regard, disaggregated by sex, are presented in Table 3.10.

Over one-fifth of the children aged 6 to 18 years in Rewasi were *working children*: 18 per cent of girls and 23 per cent of boys were working, even in terms of the narrow definition adopted here. In fact this is an undercount, since many of the girls listed as not working by our definition were engaged in household chores and care functions. Nearly one-fifth of the girls and 6.3 per cent of the boys were not attending school. If we take only the 6 to 14 years age-group, there were nine girls and eleven boys engaged in work. Except for two girls and one boy who worked for an employer outside the household, these children worked on household operational holdings.

Working children in Rewasi were drawn from all social groups with the exception of Meenas, who are classified as a Scheduled Tribe but are much better off than the general Scheduled Tribe population in India. Not a single child from among the Meenas was working at the time of our survey.

Not one child aged 6 years or less attended the *anganwadi* centre in the village at the time of our survey. Though the centre existed and a designated

Table 3.10 *School attendance among children aged 6 to 18 years, by sex and work status, Rewasi, 2010* (number and per cent)

| Children | No. | Not attending school | | | | Attending school | | | |
| | | Not working | | Working | | Not working | | Working | |
		No.	%	No.	%	No.	%	No.	%
Girls	222	27	12.2	16	7.2	166	74.8	13	5.8
Boys	224	4	1.8	10	4.5	162	72.3	48	21.4
All	446	31	7.0	26	5.8	328	73.5	61	13.7

Note: Work (in all references in this chapter) is defined as three specific types of activities: (a) work outside the household for an employer (paid and unpaid); (b) work on household operational holding; (c) work in any household enterprise other than animal resources. Any person 18 years or below engaged in any of these three activities was considered to be 'working'.
Source: Survey data.

anganwadi worker had been posted, in our survey, no child was reported to be attending the *anganwadi*. On the day of a follow-up visit in 2011, we found twenty children (or less than 20 per cent of the children in the age-group 3 to 6 years) at the *anganwadi* centre.

Literacy

The PARI survey categorised respondents in terms of literacy, not in a binary manner as literate/non-literate but in four categories: cannot read or write; can only sign name; can read but not write; can read and write – and it is only the last category that we treat as literate in the discussion that follows.

Table 3.11 presents the distribution of the population of Rewasi aged 7 years and above by sex and level of literacy. The literacy rate in Rewasi for the population aged 7 years and older was 59.8 per cent. This overall rate masks a huge difference in literacy rates between males and females. The female literacy rate, at 46 per cent, was 30 percentage points lower than the male literacy rate, which stood at 76 per cent. The literacy rate for rural Rajasthan as per the 2011 Census was 62.3 per cent (males 77.5 per cent, females 46.2 per cent), while the rural literacy rate for Sikar district was 86.4 per cent for males and 56.7 per cent for females. On the face of it, it would appear that Rewasi's performance was close to the State average and well below that of Sikar. However, one must bear in mind that census literacy rates tend to be overestimates.

Table 3.11 *Distribution of population (7 years and above), by literacy level, by sex, Rewasi, 2010*

Literacy status	Female		Male		Persons	
	No.	%	No.	%	No.	%
Cannot read and write	243	40.6	79	15.7	322	29.2
Can only sign name	78	13.0	35	6.9	113	10.2
Can read but cannot write	2	0.3	6	1.2	8	0.7
Can read and write	276	46.1	384	76.2	660	59.8
All	599	100.0	504	100.0	1103	100.0

Source: Survey data.

Table 3.12 *Proportion of literates in the population (7 years and above), by sex and socio-economic class, Rewasi, 2010*

Socio-economic class	Women	Men	Persons
Landlords and rural rich	59.1	89.5	73.2
Peasant: 1	44.7	75.6	59.1
Peasant: 2	48.7	75.7	61.5
Peasant: 3	45.6	74.8	58.4
Peasant: 4	46.2	74.5	58.5
Hired workers	42.7	69.5	55.1
Artisan work and work at traditional caste calling	66.7	83.3	73.3
Business activity/self-employed	45.8	100	78.3
Salaried person/s	48	100	79
Pensions and handouts	0	0	0
All	46.1	76.2	59.8

Source: Survey data.

The large disparity in literacy levels of men and women was seen across all classes. Among landlord and rural rich households, only 59 per cent of women were literate, while the literacy rate among men was about 90 per cent (Table 3.12).

Let us now turn to literacy rates of the adult population. One would expect these to be generally lower than the 7-plus rates, since a large majority of persons between the ages of 7 and 18 years would be currently in school and literate. Among males, the literacy rate for adults, at 66 per cent, was a little

Table 3.13 *Population who can read and write, by age cohorts, by sex, Rewasi, 2010*

Age group	Number			Literacy rate		
	Female	Male	Persons	Female	Male	Persons
6 to 17 years	160	180	340	77.7	88.7	83.1
18 to 34 years	106	116	222	53.3	89.2	67.5
35 to 49 years	8	52	60	8.0	61.2	32.4
50 to 65 years	3	30	33	5.0	47.6	26.8
> 65 years	0	13	13	0.0	31.7	14.4
All	277	391	668	45.1	74.9	58.8

Source: Survey data.

higher than for the 7 plus population, but among females the literacy rates for adults was much lower, at 29 per cent.

Next, we take a look at literacy rates by age cohorts. The numbers in Table 3.13 on literacy by age cohorts bring out the fact that the big gains in female literacy are of much more recent origin than is the case with male literacy. The female literacy rates in the population of age 35 years or older were in single digit numbers. A big jump in female school attendance seems to have happened about twenty-five years ago. This also seems to be the case for males. Although male literacy rates were consistently higher than those for females, a big jump in literacy rates occurred when one moved from the age-group of 35 to 49 years to the age-group of 18 to 34 years for both males and females. While male literacy rates showed hardly any difference between the age-group of 18 to 34 years and that of 6 to 17 years, the female literacy rate for the age-group of 6 to 17 years was much higher than that for the age-group of 18 to 34 years.

Years of Schooling

A useful measure of adult achievement with respect to school education is the median years of schooling in a group. The median years of schooling for women above the age of 16 in Rewasi was zero, and this was so irrespective of social group and class.

Differences as between males and females were much larger than differences across social groups or classes when it came to median or mean years of formal education. The picture among males was not especially impressive: the median years of schooling was seven years. There were, of course, class

Table 3.14 *Median number of completed years of schooling for population above 16 years, by sex and socio-economic class, Rewasi, 2010*

Socio-economic class	Women	Men	Persons
Landlords and rural rich	0	8	5
Peasant: 1	0	5	2
Peasant: 2	0	8	4
Peasant: 3	0	5	0
Peasant: 4	0	6	0
Hired workers	0	5	0
Artisan work and work at traditional caste calling	0	0	0
Business activity/self-employed	0	10	8
Salaried person/s	0	0	0
Pensions and handouts	0	3	0
All	0	7	1

Source: Survey data.

differences, with Hired workers reporting a median of five years, and men in business households and landlord households reporting a median of ten and eight years respectively (Table 3.14).

Educational Achievement

Let us now turn to educational achievements of the population across various social groups. We begin with the number of persons who have obtained an undergraduate degree, which requires, at a minimum, fifteen completed years of schooling. We confine ourselves to the population aged 25 years or older.

There was only one female graduate in the population of Rewasi aged 25 years and above: Kamla, 27 years old, was a post-graduate and belonged to a landlord family. In this age-group, there were 330 females in Rewasi in 2010. Among the 256 males in the 25-plus age-group, there were only fourteen graduates. Clearly, for the people of Rewasi, getting a college degree is close to being a rare event. Within this picture of little achievement, it is interesting to note that four out of the fourteen male graduates belonged to Scheduled Castes.

Let us consider a still more modest measure of educational achievement, that is, the number and percentage of males, females and persons aged 25 years or older in Rewasi who had completed ten years of schooling.

Only five out of 330 females aged 25 years or older in Rewasi had completed ten years of formal schooling. The corresponding figure of forty-eight out of 256 for males in the same age-group or less than 20 per cent was not something to write home about either. All five females and more than half of the forty-eight males belonged to OBC households.

LAND OWNERSHIP, IRRIGATION AND TENURIAL RELATIONS

The distribution of land in Rewasi was characterised by low levels of landlessness, but substantial inequality in ownership and operational holdings. Only 4 per cent of households in Rewasi owned no agricultural land. However, a majority of the households owned and operated holdings that were less than 5 acres in size. Almost 80 per cent of households had operational holdings of 5 acres or less. On the other hand, four households owned and operated holdings that were larger than 25 acres in size. The largest ownership holding in the village was about 45 acres, and the largest operational holding was 32 acres.

The Access Index in Table 3.17 shows that the share of landlords and rural rich in total ownership holdings was over four times their share in the number of households. In contrast, the share of poor peasants (Peasants 4) and Hired workers in land owned was less than half their share in the total number of households. Across social groups, Jat and Brahman households owned a disproportionately high share of land, while Meena and Dalit households owned a disproportionately low share of land.

Rewasi was a village with very limited access to irrigation. There were no public sources of irrigation, and irrigation was dependent entirely on private control over groundwater extraction. Only irrigated land could be cultivated in the rabi season. Given high summer temperatures and sandy soils, irrigation was not used in the kharif season except in conditions of shortfall of monsoon rains, to protect fodder crops on small plots of land. Irrigation was done through sprinklers as flooding fields of sandy soil would have been wasteful. In the rabi season, this typically meant working in wet fields on cold winter nights to shift the sprinklers.

Table 3.19 shows that in the kharif season, irrigation was used only on 27 per cent of operational holdings. About 44 per cent of operational holdings were sown with crops without any irrigation, and 28 per cent of operational holdings were left fallow. In the rabi season, only irrigated land amounting to

Table 3.15 *Distribution of ownership holdings of land, by size-class of holding, Rewasi, 2010* (per cent and acres)

Size-class of ownership holding	Proportion of households	Proportion of ownership holding	Average size of ownership holding
Landless	4.1	0.0	0.0
Up to 2.5 acres	25.6	6.1	1.4
2.5–5 acres	27.4	16.7	3.5
5–10 acres	29.2	35.7	7.0
10–25 acres	12.3	33.0	15.2
More than 25 acres	1.4	8.4	34.7
All households	100.0	100.0	5.7

Source: Survey data.

Table 3.16 *Distribution of operational holdings of land, by size-class of holding, Rewasi, 2010* (per cent and acres)

Size-class of operational holding	Proportion of households	Proportion of operational holding	Average size of operational holding
Landless	4.1	0.0	0.0
Up to 2.5 acres	22.4	5.3	1.4
2.5-5 acres	27.9	16.2	3.5
5-10 acres	29.2	33.7	7.0
10-25 acres	14.6	35.5	14.7
More than 25 acres	1.8	9.3	30.7
All households	100	100.0	6

Source: Survey data.

49 per cent of operational holdings was sown and the rest of the land was left fallow.

Given the scarcity of rain and limited availability of irrigation, ownership of tubewells and powered open wells – which was dependent on a landowner being able to get an electricity connection and make the requisite investment – was central to the nature of control over the agricultural production system in the village. Since only irrigated lands could be cultivated in the rabi season

Table 3.17 *Distribution of ownership and operational holdings of land and Access Index across selected socio-economic classes, Rewasi, 2010* (per cent)

Socio-economic class	House-holds	Land owned	Access Index (ownership holding)	Land operated	Access Index (operational holding)
Landlords and rural rich	3.7	16.4	4.43	13.1	3.54
Peasants 1	6.4	16.3	2.55	15.2	2.37
Peasants 2	11.9	18.1	1.52	19.3	1.62
Peasants 3	26.9	27.6	1.03	28	1.04
Peasants 4	24.2	11.2	0.46	11.4	0.47
Hired workers	17.8	6.8	0.38	9.1	0.51
Salaried person/s	5.5	2.5	0.45	2.9	0.53
Others	3.7	1	0.27	1	0.27
All households	100	100	100	100	100

Source: Survey data.

Table 3.18 *Distribution of ownership and operational holding of land and Access Index across social groups, Rewasi, 2010* (per cent)

Social group	House-holds	Land owned	Access Index (ownership holding)	Land operated	Access Index (operational holding)
Brahmans	1.9	2.7	1.42	3.1	1.63
Rajputs	39.4	37.5	0.95	38.4	0.97
Jats	30.1	40.8	1.36	38.2	1.27
Dalits	9.7	7.1	0.73	5	0.52
Meenas	9.7	5.2	0.54	6.4	0.66

Source: Survey data.

and large amounts of land were left fallow owing to lack of water, control over water became a critical factor in determining who operated land and how land was used.

The distribution of irrigated land across socio-economic classes, by season, shown in Table 3.20 reveals that rich peasants and the rural rich had control over sources of irrigation.

Table 3.19 *Share of irrigated, unirrigated and fallow land in total operational holdings, by crop season, Rewasi, 2009–10* (per cent)

Season	Irrigated	Unirrigated	Fallow
Kharif	27	44	28
Rabi	49	0	51

Source: Survey data.

Table 3.20 *Distribution of households, irrigated operational holdings and total operational holdings, by selected socio-economic classes, Rewasi, 2009–10* (per cent)

Socio-economic class	Households	Irrigated land (kharif)	Irrigated land (rabi)	Total land
Landlords and rural rich	3.7	19.3	15.5	13.1
Peasants 1	6.4	20.2	17.9	15.2
Peasants 2	11.9	23.5	23.1	19.3
Peasants 3	26.9	21.9	23.2	28
Peasants 4	24.2	9.9	12.9	11.4
Hired workers	17.8	4.1	4.4	9.1
Salaried person/s	5.5	1.1	2.5	2.9
Others	3.7	0	0.4	1
All households	100	100	100	100

Source: Survey data.

Tenancy

Tenancy was not very widespread in Rewasi. Table 3.21 shows that 12 per cent of operational holdings were leased in and 14 per cent of ownership holdings were leased out. About 20 per cent of households leased in land for cultivation.

Land was leased in on annual as well as seasonal contracts. Of the total land leased in, about 48 per cent was leased in on annual contracts and the rest on seasonal contracts. Unirrigated land – which was cultivated only in the kharif season when risk of crop failure was high – was leased on sharecropping contracts. Irrigated land was leased on both fixed-rent and sharecropping contracts (Table 3.22). As might be expected, landlords and richer sections of the peasantry primarily leased land on fixed-rent contracts, while poorer sections of the peasantry and Hired workers leased in land on share-rents (Table 3.23).

Given the vital importance of irrigation, land was sometimes leased in by

Table 3.21 *Extent of leasing in and leasing out of land, Rewasi, 2009–10* (per cent)

Indicator	Per cent
Land leased in as a proportion of total operational holdings	12
Tenant households as a proportion of all households	18.7
Tenant households as a proportion of cultivator households	19.5
Land leased out as a proportion of total ownership holdings	14.3
Lessor households as a proportion of all households	17.6
Lessor households as a proportion of all landowning households	18.4

Source: Survey data.

Table 3.22 *Distribution of land leased in and land leased out across different types of contracts, Rewasi, 2009–10* (per cent)

Type of tenancy	Land leased in	Land leased out
Annual fixed rent	26.9	18.2
Annual share rent	11.3	9.8
Seasonal share-rent (kharif)	27.8	24.6
Seasonal fixed-rent (rabi)	22.6	28.2
Seasonal share-rent (rabi)	11.4	19.2

Source: Survey data.

Table 3.23 *Share of land leased in under different types of contracts, by selected socio-economic classes, Rewasi, 2009–10* (per cent)

Socio-economic class	Annual fixed rent	Annual share rent	Seasonal share-rent (kharif)	Seasonal fixed-rent (rabi)	Seasonal share-rent (rabi)	Total
Landlords and rural rich	100	0	0	0	0	100
Peasants 1	16.6	0	33.4	50.1	0	100
Peasants 2	46.4	0	21.9	31.7	0	100
Peasants 3	15.5	22.4	6.9	27.5	27.7	100
Peasants 4	0	0	31.6	39.8	28.6	100
Hired workers	3.2	29.6	64	0	3.2	100
Salaried person/s	0	7.3	20	18.2	54.5	100

Source: Survey data.

landlords and richer sections of the peasantry, who owned surplus unirrigated land that was left fallow during the rabi season, not for cultivation but for using water from tubewells/open wells on the leased-in land. In such cases, tenants left the leased-in land fallow but used water from the tubewell/open well installed on it to irrigate another plot of land. In some cases, owners of tubewells who did not have enough land leased in unirrigated land at low rents to cultivate with water from their tubewells. Rent for leasing in unirrigated land was less than the cost of buying irrigation water from tubewell owners. While very few tubewell owners had surplus water that they were willing to provide for payment, land for lease was easily available to those who had access to water. Land could be rented under a fixed-rent contract for about 1.4 quintals of wheat per acre for cultivating wheat in the rabi season, while a tubewell owner charged at least 4.5 quintals of wheat per acre for providing water for irrigation.

There were eleven functional open wells in the village. Traditionally, eight families had equal right to irrigation from each of these wells. With the partitioning of households and land, some of these shares have also been subdivided. The open wells now have deeper tubewells at the base and electric pumps for extraction of water. Water from these wells is used to irrigate an equal extent of land (or a fraction when the water rights have been subdivided due to partitioning of households) in the rabi season. In some cases, households leased land from other partners to gain additional right to irrigation from the well.

WEALTH INEQUALITY

Distribution of non-land assets, in particular, means of production, non-agricultural land and assets related to non-agricultural businesses, was extremely unequal in Rewasi. As a result, distribution of overall wealth in Rewasi was more unequal than the distribution of land.

Table 3.24 shows that the top decile of households owned 38 per cent of total assets or wealth. On the other hand, the bottom 50 per cent of households owned only 19 per cent of total assets.

The distribution of assets across classes (Table 3.25) shows that landlords and the rural rich, who constituted 4 per cent of all households, owned 20 per cent of all assets. They controlled all forms of assets: 18 per cent of the value of agricultural land and trees, 26 per cent in the case of other land and buildings, 35 per cent in the case of other means of production, and 38 per cent in the case of means of transport. By contrast, Hired workers, who constituted

18 per cent of all households, owned 7 per cent of total assets (and 10 per cent of animal wealth in the village).

Table 3.26 shows the composition of assets for each socio-economic class in terms of the average value of a particular asset owned by households in a given class, as well as the composition of assets of households in that class. We observe that for all categories of assets – land, animal resources, means of production and so on – the average value of assets owned by landlords was the highest, followed by rich peasants (Peasants 1 and 2), then poor peasants (Peasants 3 and 4), and finally, Hired workers. To take the case of land, on average, a landlord household owned land valued at Rs 33 lakhs as compared to a Peasant 4 household, whose land assets were valued at less than Rs 3 lakhs. Hired workers owned animals worth around Rs 20,000 while rich peasants owned animals worth Rs 70,000, and so on.

In terms of the composition of assets, land was the most important asset for rich peasants and for peasants in general. For Hired workers, agricultural land as well as other land and buildings were important components of total assets. Animal resources accounted for a slightly higher proportion of the total assets of Hired workers than of peasant households.

Table 3.24 *Distribution of wealth across deciles of asset holding, Rewasi, 2010* (Rs and per cent)

Decile of wealth	Total wealth (Rs)	Share in total (per cent)
D1	3519,670	1
D2	7410,165	3
D3	10738,575	4
D4	13585,374	5
D5	16734,055	6
D6	20179,219	7
D7	24326,462	8
D8	34427,264	12
D9	50083,489	16
D10	115481,058	38

Source: Survey data.

Table 3.25 *Distribution of wealth by type of asset across selected socio-economic classes, Rewasi, 2010* (per cent)

Socio-economic class	Agricultural land and trees	Other land and buildings	Animals	Other means of production	Means of transport	All means of production	Other assets	All assets
Landlord and rural rich	18	26	12	35	28	21	12	20
Peasant: 1	22	8	10	16	4	21	12	17
Peasant: 2	20	17	20	16	29	19	18	19
Peasant: 3	23	16	28	19	14	21	21	21
Peasant: 4	9	16	15	7	6	8	20	11
Hired workers	6	8	10	4	3	6	12	7
Business activity/ self-employed	1	4	1	0	15	1	1	2
Other households	2	4	5	2	1	2	4	3
All households	100	100	100	100	100	100	100	100

Source: Survey data.

Table 3.26 *Average values of assets in different asset categories, by selected socio-economic classes, Rewasi, 2010 (Rs and per cent)*

Socio-economic class	Agricultural land and trees		Other land and buildings		Animals		Other means of production		Means of transport		Domestic durables		Other assets		All assets	
	Rupees	Per cent	Rupees	Per cent	Rupees	Per cent	Rupees	Per cent	Rupees	Per cent	Rupees	Per cent	Rupees	Per cent	Rupees	Per cent
Landlord and rural rich	3314539	44	3055000	40	138912	2	368540	5	603800	8	47788	0.6	112639	1	7414794	100
Peasant: 1	2724123	78	449833	12	69150	2	94540	2	139666	4	29448	0.8	60370	1.7	3450641	100
Peasant: 2	1213534	56	587892	26	75721	3	60157	2	282427	12	31799	1	44294	2	2103945	100
Peasant: 3	617865	62	239117	24	42696	4	41837	4	139927	14	20340	2	17960	1	992127	100
Peasant: 4	272749	47	216496	37	26699	4	17327	2	56358	9	18898	3	22702	3	580007	100
Hired workers	233008	48	170034	35	22882	4	19845	4	39787	8	15794	3	19483	4	477025	100
All households	745452	55	387342	27	42974	3	54948	3	195818	13	21599	1	28193	2	1298079	100

Note: The second column for each asset category shows the percentage share of the specific asset in total asset holdings of the class.

Source: Survey data.

CROPPING PATTERN AND YIELDS

Pearl millet (*bajra*) was the most important crop of the kharif season. In 2009–10, about 28 per cent of operational holdings were sown with a stand-alone crop of pearl millet and 15 per cent of operational holdings were sown with pearl millet intercropped with various other crops. About 20 per cent of operational holdings had kharif pulses (Table 3.27). In 2009–10, kharif crops were completely destroyed on about 64 per cent of land sown during the season. Among poor peasants and Hired workers, a significant share of the kharif crop was completely destroyed, as they had very limited access to irrigation and could not save their crops (Table 3.28). In the rabi season, irrigated land was sown with wheat and barley (26 per cent of operational holdings), rapeseed (13 per cent of operational holdings), fodder crops, onions and fenugreek (Table 3.27).

District-level data on yields of crops (Figure 3.1) showed that there was a

Table 3.27 *Area under different crops as a proportion of total operational holdings and gross cropped area, Rewasi, 2009–10* (per cent)

Season	Crop	Share in gross cropped area	Share in total operational holding
Kharif	Bajra (Pearl millet)	5	28
Kharif	Kharif pulses	4	20
Kharif	Bajra and intercrops	3	15
Kharif	Kharif oilseeds	0	3
Kharif	Fodder crops	0	2
Kharif	Other kharif crops	1	3
Kharif	All kharif crops	13	72
Rabi	Wheat + Barley	4	26
Rabi	Rapeseed	2	13
Rabi	Fodder crops	1	3
Rabi	Fenugreek	0	3
Rabi	Onion	0	1
Rabi	Other rabi crops	1	3
Rabi	All rabi crops	9	49
Total	All crops	100	518

Source: Survey data.

Table 3.28 *Proportion of area sown in kharif on which crops were completely destroyed, by socio-economic class, Rewasi, 2009–10* (per cent)

Socio-economic class	Per cent
Landlords and rural rich	49
Peasants 1	44
Peasants 2	50
Peasants 3	75
Peasants 4	67
Hired workers	85
All households	64

Source: Survey data.

Figure 3.1 *Yields of major kharif crops, Sikar district, 1998–99 to 2010–11*

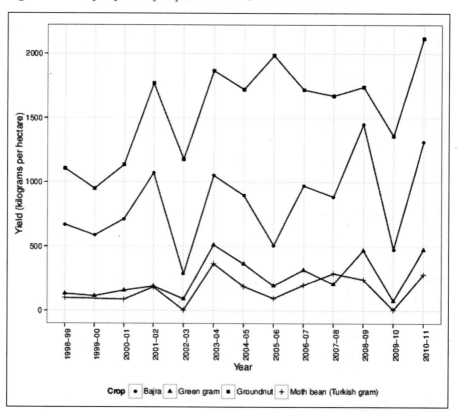

Table 3.29 *Comparison of average yield of main rabi crops in Rewasi with average yield in Sikar, Rajasthan and India, 2009–10* (kg per acre)

Level	Wheat	Barley	Rapeseed
Rewasi	1018	953	569
Sikar	1344	1148	502
Rajasthan	1113	–	480
India	1096	–	443

Source: Survey data and District-wise Crop Production Estimates, Directorate of Economics and Statistics, Ministry of Agriculture, Government of India.

Figure 3.2 *Yields of major rabi crops, Sikar district, 1998–99 to 2010–11*

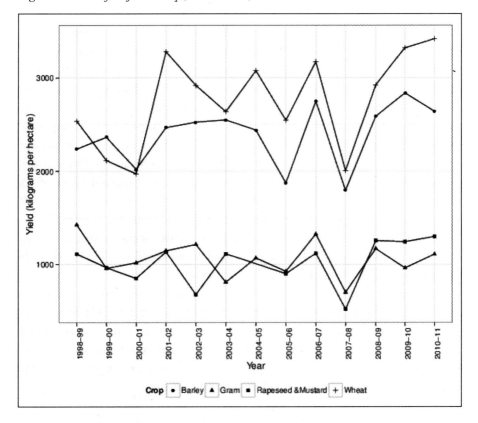

sharp fall in the yield of kharif crops in 2009–10, as compared to levels obtained the previous year.

While official statistics for yield of kharif crops showed a significant fall in 2009–10 relative to 2008–09, data for yield of rabi crops showed that there was no significant decline in 2009–10 from previous levels (Figure 3.2). Yields of rabi crops, wheat and barley in particular, in Rewasi were low, and lower than the average yields for Sikar district as a whole (Table 3.29). Table 3.29 shows that in 2009–10, the average yield of wheat in Rewasi was only 10 quintals per acre.

While pearl millet, the main crop in the kharif season, had failed almost completely, yields of rabi crops were low on account of a deficit in water availability.

COST OF CULTIVATION AND INCOME FROM CROP PRODUCTION

On account of low rainfall in 2009–10, kharif crops were destroyed and abandoned on most fields in Rewasi. However, most cultivators had incurred substantial expenditure in land preparation and sowing before the crop was abandoned. This resulted in income losses in the kharif season. Table 3.30 shows that 78 per cent of cultivators incurred a loss in the kharif season. The proportion of households that incurred a loss was 50 per cent among landlords and richer sections of the peasantry, but over 80 per cent among poorer sections of the peasantry and Hired workers (with cultivation). On average, cultivators spent Rs 1,706 per acre on kharif crops and incurred a loss of Rs 663 per acre (Table 3.30). Table 3.31 also shows that, on average, households in the top two classes (Landlords and rural rich, and Peasants 1) were able to break even by protecting some crops using their better access to irrigation. On the other hand, 'Peasants 4' and cultivators from Hired worker households incurred an average loss of over Rs 1,000 per acre.

Data for rabi crops show that the average net return was highest for wheat (Rs 10,053 per acre), followed by rapeseed (Rs 7,213 per acre). Of all the rabi crops, net returns were lowest for gram. In 2009–10, households that cultivated gram incurred, on average, a loss of Rs 1,788 per acre. While the average cost of cultivation of wheat was higher than that of rapeseed and gram, net returns for wheat were higher than for other crops on account of higher yields and value of output in the case of wheat.

A recent study based on data from the Project on Agrarian Relations in India (PARI) shows that there is a positive relationship between scale of production and returns from cultivation (Rawal and Swaminathan 2012). Data

Table 3.30 *Proportion of cultivators who incurred a loss in kharif crops, by selected socio-economic classes, Rewasi, 2009–10* (per cent)

Socio-economic class	Proportion of cultivators who incurred a loss in kharif cultivation
Landlords and rural rich	50
Peasants 1	46
Peasants 2	76
Peasants 3	81
Peasants 4	83
Hired workers	86
All households	78

Source: Survey data.

Table 3.31 *Average per acre gross value of output, cost A2 and net income from kharif cultivation by selected socio-economic classes, Rewasi, 2009–10* (Rs per acre)

Socio-economic class	Gross value of output	Cost A2	Net income
Landlords and rural rich	1781	1670	110
Peasants 1	1857	1487	370
Peasants 2	1284	1660	–376
Peasants 3	1036	1484	–448
Peasants 4	854	1924	–1070
Hired workers	626	1904	–1278
All households	1043	1706	–663

Note: Net income is defined here as gross income minus cost A2.
Source: Survey data.

from Rewasi also showed a positive relationship between scale of production and gross value of output as well as net returns to cultivation. Landlords and rich peasants used their access to irrigation and capital to obtain higher yields (Table 3.32) as well as higher net returns (Table 3.31) from rabi crops. While the average yield of wheat on land cultivated by landlords and rural rich was about 13 quintals per acre, 'Peasants 4' obtained only about 9.5 quintals per acre. Similarly, the yield of rapeseed on land cultivated by landlords and rich peasants was 7 quintals per acre, while the corresponding figure for 'Peasants

Table 3.32 *Average yield of wheat and rapeseed, by selected socio-economic classes, Rewasi, 2009–10* (kg per acre)

Socio-economic class	Wheat	Rapeseed
Landlords and rural rich	1290	700
Peasants 1	1190	543
Peasants 2	1054	553
Peasants 3	981	552
Peasants 4	943	563
Hired workers	1009	376
All households	1018	569

Source: Survey data.

Table 3.33 *Average per acre gross value of output, cost A2 and net income, by crop, Rewasi, 2009–10* (Rs per acre)

Crop	Gross value of output	Cost A2	Net income
Wheat	19077	9023	10053
Rapeseed	12873	5660	7213
Barley	11316	6715	4601
Gram	5122	6910	−1788

Source: Survey data.

Table 3.34 *Average net income per acre from cultivation of wheat and rapeseed, by selected socio-economic classes, Rewasi, 2009–10* (Rs per acre)

Socio-economic class	Wheat	Rapeseed
Landlords and rural rich	11616	8866
Peasant: 1	14197	7231
Peasant: 2	10781	6596
Peasant: 3	10371	6938
Peasant: 4	8548	6811
Hired workers	9012	4923

Source: Survey data.

4' was only about 5.6 quintals per acre and for cultivating households among Hired workers was only about 3.7 quintals per acre (Table 3.32).

Table 3.35 shows the structure of cost of cultivation of major rabi crops in Rewasi. Irrigation was the most important item in the cost of cultivation of wheat and rapeseed. Other major items of cost were machines (which were primarily used for land preparation, harvesting and threshing) and hiring of casual workers.

Table 3.36 shows average item-wise cost of wheat cultivation for households belonging to different classes. The data clearly show that poor peasants and cultivators among Hired workers were in a disadvantageous position in respect of the cost they had to incur on some major items like irrigation, seeds and deployment of machinery. For example, while landlords and the rural rich spent about Rs 1,760 per acre on irrigation, the average expenditure on irrigation incurred by households belonging to the class Peasants 4 was Rs 3,659 per acre, and the average expenditure on irrigation incurred by cultivators from the

Table 3.35 *Average cost of cultivation, by item of expenditure, by crop, rabi crops, Rewasi, 2009–10* (Rs per acre)

Item	Wheat		Rapeseed		Gram	
	Rs	%	Rs	%	Rs	%
Seeds	916	10.2	116	2.0	657	9.5
Manure	445	4.9	78	1.4	87	1.3
Chemical fertilisers	407	4.5	266	4.7	183	2.6
Plant protection chemicals	92	1.0	27	0.5	480	6.9
Irrigation	2504	27.8	1692	29.9	1628	23.6
Casual labour	1454	16.1	867	15.3	1114	16.1
Long-term labour	68	0.8	122	2.2	0	0.0
Machines	1407	15.6	1252	22.1	2282	33.0
Animals	46	0.5	11	0.2	0	0.0
Rent for leased-in land	538	6.0	355	6.3	0	0.0
Other expenses	4	0.0	26	0.5	0	0.0
Share of annual expenses	0	0.0	0	0.0	0	0.0
Total cost A2	9023	100.0	5660	100.0	6910	100.0

Source: Survey data.

Table 3.36 *Average cost of cultivation of wheat, by item of expenditure, by selected socio-economic classes, Rewasi, 2009–10* (Rs per acre)

Item	Landlords and rural rich	Peasants 1	Peasants 2	Peasants 3	Peasants 4	Hired workers
Seeds	643	839	940	949	934	1051
Manure	139	434	576	483	426	375
Chemical fertilisers	319	317	394	363	528	353
Plant protection chemicals	178	69	110	85	76	66
Irrigation	1760	2268	1726	2015	3659	3195
Casual labour	1928	1561	1651	1419	1543	754
Long-term labour	712	0	41	72	0	0
Machines	1493	1543	1440	1210	1716	1091
Animals	34	3	21	136	0	0
Rent for leased-in land	0	50	618	373	197	1434
Other expenses	0	0	23	0	0	0
Share of annual expenses	969	987	989	888	1002	1005
Total cost A2	8363	8272	8736	8184	10324	9556

Source: Survey data.

Table 3.37 *Average cost of cultivation of rapeseed, by item of expenditure, by selected socio-economic classes, Rewasi, 2009–10* (Rs per acre)

Item	Landlords and rural rich	Peasants 1	Peasants 2	Peasants 3	Peasants 4	Hired workers
Seeds	643	839	940	949	934	1051
Manure	139	434	576	483	426	375
Chemical fertilisers	319	317	394	363	528	353
Plant protection chemicals	178	69	110	85	76	66
Irrigation	1760	2268	1726	2015	3659	3195
Casual labour	1928	1561	1651	1419	1543	754
Long-term labour	712	0	41	72	0	0
Machines	1493	1543	1440	1210	1716	1091
Animals	34	3	21	136	0	0
Rent for leased-in land	0	50	618	373	197	1434
Other expenses	0	0	23	0	0	0
Share of annual expenses	969	987	989	888	1002	1005
Total cost A2	8363	8272	8736	8184	10324	9556

Source: Survey data.

class of Hired workers was Rs 3,195 per acre. Average expenditure on seeds was Rs 643 per acre for landlords and rural rich, while it was Rs 934 per acre for households belonging to the class Peasants 4 and Rs 1,051 per acre for households belonging to the class of Hired workers. As expected, households belonging to Peasants 4 and Hired worker classes saved on costs of hiring workers since they deployed more family labour on their fields than landlords and richer sections of peasantry did.

A similar pattern of class-wise variation was seen in cost of cultivation data for rapeseed (Table 3.37).

Box 1: Farm Harvest Price and MSP

We computed the weighted average farm harvest price (FHP) of wheat and compared it with the minimum support price (MSP) for cultivators in Rewasi. The average FHP was Rs 1,319 for 100 kg of wheat in Rewasi in 2009–10, which was higher than the announced support price of Rs 1,080 in that year. Further, all wheat producers in Rewasi received prices higher than the MSP announced by the central government. However, there was a Rs 200 per quintal difference in prices received across cultivators.

One reason for the FHP being higher than the centrally announced MSP of wheat in Rewasi was that the State government gave a bonus that year. The State government bonus seems justified if we go by costs

Figure 1 *Distribution of cost (A2+FL) per 100 kg of wheat in Rewasi village, Rajasthan, 2009–10*

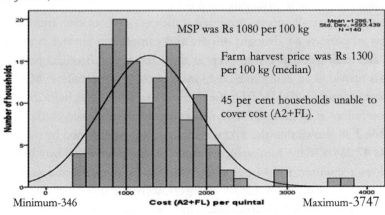

of cultivation, as the costs for a majority of cultivators in Rewasi were higher than the all-India average. Figure 1 shows the variation in costs across households: from Rs 346 to Rs 3747 per 100 kg of wheat. Centrally announced MSP did not cover the costs of more than half of all wheat producers in Rewasi. Even the actual farm harvest price failed to cover costs of cultivation of 45 per cent of cultivators (accounting for 28 per cent of production). Costs here included imputed value of family labour.

Not only that, this variation in costs across wheat producers was such that costs rose as we moved from rich to middle to poor peasants. Costs of production were higher for Peasant 4 households (Rs 1376 per quintal) as compared to Peasant 1 households (Rs 923 per quintal). The average cost of production per quintal of wheat in this village (Rs 1251) was higher than the official State level average (Rs 451 per quintal), which may be because of lower productivity of wheat in the village due to serious water shortages in the reference year.

Source: Biplab Sarkar.

ANIMAL RESOURCES IN REWASI

Animals had an extremely crucial role to play in the household economy of Rewasi. All households in Rewasi owned some animals: buffaloes, cows, goats or camels. Camels, mainly females, were used as the main draught animal in the village. Goats were primarily used for milk.

Animals, especially goats, provided a means of economic and nutritional security in periods of drought. Goats and camels can survive on leaves of *khejri* and *aadu* trees, available even in the harshest of drought years. These animals provided an economic cushion in years of crop failure. Milch cattle, by contrast, require fodder from field crops like wheat and bajra. So, in years of crop failure, it became difficult and expensive to maintain cattle.

Table 3.38 shows that the average value of animals owned by a household was Rs 47,264. Of the total value of stock of animals owned by a household, buffaloes accounted for 44 per cent, cows for 22 per cent and goats for 23 per cent of animal wealth. Goats, however, were the most commonly owned animals: 94 per cent of all households in Rewasi kept goats at the time of our survey.

The pattern of ownership of animals, by type, across socio-economic classes (Table 3.39) clearly shows that poorer households belonging to the poorer sections of peasants and Hired workers owned mainly goats. On the other land, landlords and richer sections of the peasantry owned goats, camels and cattle. Since households belonging to landlord and richer sections of the peasantry had substantial amounts of land and access to some irrigation, they could obtain fodder for maintaining cattle. By contrast, very few households among poor peasants and Hired workers maintained cattle because of lack of reliable access to fodder.

Further, Table 3.40 shows that the average value of animal holdings – of cattle, goats and all animals – declined sharply as we moved from landlords and richer sections of the peasantry towards poorer sections of the peasantry and Hired workers. It may be noted that some Hired worker households maintained camels and camel carts to transport different kinds of materials (farm produce, inputs, fodder, sand, bricks and other goods) on rent (Table 3.39).

Table 3.38 *Average value of animals per household, by type of animal, Rewasi, 2009–10* (Rs and per cent of total)

Type of animal	Value per household	Percentage of total
Buffaloes	29,483	44
Cows	19,415	22
Camels	27,352	6
Goats	11,597	23
Other animals	5,688	5
All animals	47,264	100

Source: Survey data.

Table 3.39 *Proportion of households that owned different types of animals, by selected socio-economic classes, Rewasi, 2009–10* (per cent)

Socio-economic class	Camels	Milch cattle	Goats	Sheep
Landlords and rural rich	25	100	88	25
Peasants 1 and 2	25	98	98	10
Peasants 3 and 4	5	83	93	10
Hired workers	10	59	97	13

Source: Survey data.

Table 3.40 *Average value of animals per household, by type of animal, by selected socio-economic classes, Rewasi, 2009–10* (Rs)

Socio-economic class	Cows/Buffaloes	Goats	All animals
Landlords and rural rich	101875	17821	139000
Peasants 1	54893	12664	74629
Peasants 2	59040	13650	81290
Peasants 3	32196	12475	49719
Peasants 4	24511	10506	30599
Hired workers	20967	10122	26146
Salaried person/s	32473	8725	39225
Others	13000	8583	13714

Source: Survey data.

Table 3.41 *Output from maintenance of animal resources, by selected socio-economic classes, Rewasi, 2009–10* (Rs per household)

Socio-economic class	Gross value of output
Landlords and rural rich	141877
Peasants 1	71885
Peasants 2	89831
Peasants 3	49780
Peasants 4	34881
Hired workers	23859
All households	49463

Source: Survey data.

Turning to incomes from animal resources, Table 3.41 shows that average gross value of output from animals for a household declined sharply as one moved from landlords and richer sections of the peasantry to poor peasants and Hired workers. Average annual gross value of output of animals for a land-lord/rural rich household was about Rs 1.4 lakhs, whereas the corresponding annual gross value of output for a Hired worker household was only Rs 23,859.

Table 3.42 brings out some important points in respect of the economics of animal resources. First, it shows that households in Rewasi derived substantial income – on average, Rs 23,114 per annum – from animals. Secondly, the

Table 3.42 *Average income and expenditure on maintenance of animal resources, by selected socio-economic classes, Rewasi, 2009–10* (Rs per household)

Socio-economic class	Gross value of output (1)	Value of home-grown fodder (2)	Expenditure on purchased feed/fodder (3)	Total expenses (4)	Net income (col. 1 – col. 4)
Landlords and rural rich	141877	28901	31667	67217	74661
Peasants 1	71885	21198	20005	41678	29307
Peasants 2	89831	21880	17616	41649	48126
Peasants 3	49780	9044	18155	28801	20978
Peasants 4	34881	5575	12429	18409	16472
Hired workers	23859	4340	7903	12561	11298
All households	49463	9885	15181	26285	23114

Source: Survey data.

data show that net income from animal resources declined as one went from landlord/rural rich households to households of poorer peasants and Hired workers. Thirdly, purchased commodities (fodder, feed) constituted the most important item of cost in the maintenance of animals. It is important to note that the expenditure on purchasing feed/fodder for animals was likely to be higher than 'income' on account of lack of crop fodder in a year of drought.

Since fodder, the most important constituent of the cost of maintenance of animals, was common to all animals in a household, it was not possible for us to separately calculate incomes for each type of animal. However, data on output and costs across households with different kind of animal holdings suggest that in a year of low rainfall, and consequent crop failure, households that owned cattle faced severe economic stress in maintaining the animals. Not only was the quantity of home-grown fodder and availability of fodder in the market severely restricted in such a year, but the cost of growing fodder crops rose steeply (because of the high cost of irrigation) and so did the price of fodder in the market. In 2009–10, net incomes from cows and buffaloes were relatively low because of the high expenditure incurred in growing and purchasing fodder.

Goats, by contrast, provided an important cushion during periods of economic stress. Goats feed on leaves of *khejri* and *aadu* trees, which are available even during periods of drought. The strategy of households in Rewasi was to

Table 3.43 *Number and value of goats and goat kids sold during 2009–10 as a proportion of number and value of goats and goat kids owned, by selected socio-economic classes, Rewasi, 2009–10* (per cent)

Socio-economic class	Number of animals sold as a proportion of total animals	Value of animals sold as a proportion of total value of animals
Landlords and rural rich	35	21
Peasants 1	23	16
Peasants 2	27	22
Peasants 3	21	14
Peasants 4	26	18
Hired workers	19	12
All households	24	16

Source: Survey data.

build a stock of goats in normal agricultural years and sell their ovine holdings in years of drought. Table 3.43 shows that a quarter of goats/goat kids owned by households in Rewasi were sold during the survey year.

HOUSEHOLD INCOMES

Estimates of household income show that the mean income of a household in Rewasi was Rs 23,705 in 2009–10, and the median income, as expected, was lower at Rs 15,951. The proportion of households with a per capita income of less than two dollars a day (at purchasing power parity), the international poverty line, was 49 per cent. In other words, one-half of all households were income-poor in the survey year.

Inequality in incomes was marked with a substantial concentration of income in the hands of households belonging to the class of landlords and rural rich. On the other hand, the poorest peasants and Hired workers had a disproportionately low share in the total income. Table 3.47 shows that landlords and rural rich, who comprised just 4 per cent of households, accounted for about 21 per cent of total income (of resident households). The next three classes, that is, the top three peasant classes, had a share in income that was very close to their share in the number of households. Peasants 4 households accounted for about 21 per cent of households but only 13 per cent of income. Similarly, Hired workers accounted for 16 per cent of households but only 9 per cent of income.

In 2009–10, the average annual income of a household belonging to the landlord and rural rich class was over Rs 8 lakhs. On the other hand, the average income of a household belonging to the class of Hired workers was Rs 74,027. The average for all households was Rs 1.4 lakhs. It is interesting to note that total household income of the two richest households in the village was about Rs 50 lakhs. To put it differently, a landlord household obtained, on average, an income that was ten times that obtained by a Hired worker household.

An interesting finding from our survey is the diversification of income sources (see Box 2). On average, a household received income from four different sources. Poorer households were dependent on agriculture-based incomes, whereas richer households had diversified into non-agricultural businesses.

Incomes from crop production were remarkably low in Rewasi: total income from crop production of all cultivator households was Rs 36 lakhs or 11 per cent of the total household income of residents of the village.

Income from trees was an important part of the income of cultivators in Rewasi (Table 3.48). Of total agricultural income, about 25 per cent came from trees and the rest from seasonal crops. The most important tree crop in Rewasi was *khejri* (*Prosopis cineraria*).[3] Scores of *khejri* trees marked the landscape of the village; they were planted on fields as well as on public land. *Khejri* trees were a crucial source of fodder for goats and camels, particularly in summer when all other sources of fodder became extremely scarce. Given their great economic utility in maintaining the animal resources of the village, *khejri* trees were greatly valued. *Khejri* leaves were harvested once a year, around October–November. The branches were cut and dried. The dried leaves (*loong*), about 30–35 kilograms of which were produced per year per tree, were then removed and stored for use as fodder for goats and camels. Dried twigs were used as fuel.

Non-agricultural occupations were important sources of income in Rewasi. About 45 per cent of the total income of all households came from non-agricultural businesses. Non-agricultural businesses accounted for 65 per cent of incomes of landlords and the rural rich, and a substantial share of income of all categories of peasants.

Remittances were an important source of household incomes in Rewasi. Of the 219 households in the village, 87 households (or 40 per cent) were

---

[3] In addition, leaves of the *aadu* (local name, English and botanical names not known) tree were also fed to goats. However, since there was no market price for *aadu* leaves, these have not been valued in the calculation of incomes.

'migrant' households, that is, households with at least one current migrant (Thomas and Das 2014).[4] Migrants comprised around 10 per cent of the total population of Rewasi, and 96 per cent of the migrants were males who had migrated for employment-related reasons. The proportion of all remittance-receiving households, however, was higher, at 52 per cent.[5] The total remittances received during the survey year were Rs 69 lakhs, amounting to 22 per cent of total household incomes. On average, a household in Rewasi received Rs 31,176 a year as remittances. Table 3.44 shows that a substantial proportion of households in all classes received remittances.

Of those who migrated and sent remittances, a quarter were outside the country and 60 per cent were in other States of the country (Table 3.45).

The average annual income and the average per capita income of a migrant household was 29 per cent higher than that of a non-migrant household (Table 3.46). Housing conditions of migrant households were better than that of non-migrant households: the houses of 45 per cent of migrant households had functional latrines, as compared to only 25 per cent of non-migrant households. Also, authorised electricity and separate kitchens were more prevalent in migrant households than in non-migrant households.

Table 3.44 *Proportion of households that received migrant remittances, by selected socio-economic classes, Rewasi, 2009–10* (per cent)

Socio-economic class	Proportion of households
Landlords and rural rich	50
Peasants 1	21
Peasants 2	23
Peasants 3	56
Peasants 4	39
Hired workers	50
Business activity/self-employed	50
All households	42

Source: Survey data.

[4] Current migrants are defined as members of a household who were not present in the village for six months or more during the survey year.
[5] While calculating remittances all types of remittances were taken into account, i.e. regardless of whether the concerned household was currently a migrant household.

Table 3.45 *Number of household members who migrated and sent remittances, by destination, Rewasi, 2009–10* (number and percentage of total)

Destination of migrants	Number	Share of total
Within Sikar district	5	4
To other districts of Rajasthan	12	11
To States other than Rajasthan	66	61
To any other country	26	24
Total	109	100

Source: Survey data.

Table 3.46 *Average income of migrant and non-migrant households, Rewasi, 2009–10* (Rs)

Type of household	Average household income	Average per capita income
Migrant households	1,65,609	27,335
Non-migrant households	1,28,526	21,313

Source: Survey data.

Table 3.47 *Average household and per capita income, by socio-economic class, Rewasi, 2009–10* (Rs)

Socio-economic class	Household income	Per capita income
Landlords and rural rich	809273	77173
Peasants 1	188665	28093
Peasants 2	171060	29707
Peasants 3	121236	22488
Peasants 4	76990	18568
Hired workers	74027	14566
Artisanal work and work at traditional caste calling	25347	6129
Business activity/self-employed	1015469	79633
Salaried person/s	126194	25996
Pensions and handouts	22890	13278
All households	143258	23705

Source: Survey data.

Table 3.48 *Average income from different sources, by socio-economic class, Rewasi, 2009–10* (Rs per household)

Socio-economic class	Crop production	Income from trees	Rent from agricultural land	Agricultural labour	Non-agricultural labour	Salaries	Business and self-employment	Pensions and remittances	Other sources
Landlords and rural rich	166522	23322	63274	–	3454	21000	894958	138750	76464
Peasant: 1	97199	13690	4957	8143	6242	12000	84820	88250	27176
Peasant: 2	76801	8070	7164	11598	5934	39200	103760	90000	12467
Peasant: 3	33606	6335	11330	10754	15253	24333	89150	78213	11758
Peasant: 4	22120	2303	–1,183*	7455	6498	22000	40917	78718	1563
Hired workers	13593	1993	4737	18230	21302	86120	8400	38167	700
Artisan work and work at traditional caste calling	–6,050	–	–	1190	5500	–	35000	–	15667
Business activity/ self-employed	5896	6174	–	–	–	9000	851500	147400	–
Salaried person/s	24003	2586	1655	3115	7967	89346	60900	–	3000
Pensions and handouts	1645	630	–	–	–	–	–	22900	9475
All households	39806	5710	17869	12943	13397	57199	199646	75754	20345

Note: *One household which had leased-out land on sharing basis incurred losses.
Source: Survey data.

Box 2: Diversification of Incomes

Diversification of incomes at the household level is measured here by computing the inverse Herfindahl–Hirschman index of market concentration (HHI).[6] This commonly used index combines diversity in terms of the number of sources of income and the income share of each source. The index is defined as the inverse of the sum of squares of shares of each source of income. An index value of 1 represents a case where the household specialises in any one source of income, and a value higher than one indicates more diversified income portfolios. This index is calculated for each household and then averaged for the group. As we have used ten categories of income, the inverse HHI value will range between 1 and 10.

We have used the following ten-fold classification of sources of income:
- Crop production (including tree crops)
- Animal husbandry
- Agricultural wages
- Non-agricultural wages
- Salaries
- Non-agricultural self-employment
- Rent from agricultural land
- Rent from machinery and other assets
- Pensions, remittances and transfers
- Any other source

In Rewasi, on average, a household reported 3.8 sources of income (the maximum number being 8). A negligible proportion, 0.5 per cent, of households obtained incomes from only one source. Around 80 per cent of the households received incomes from 2 to 4 sources (Table 1). The inverse Herfindahl–Hirschman index value was 2.38, reflecting the fact that most households obtained more than one source of income.

To understand the relationship between income levels and income diversification, we examined the nature of income diversification among the poorest 40 per cent of households and the richest 10 per cent of households (ranked by per capita household income).

Relatively poor households, that is, those in the lowest 40 per cent of the income distribution, relied more on agriculture than the rich, that is, those in the top 10 per cent of the income distribution. Non-agricultural sources of income accounted for 84 per cent of the total income of the richest households of Rewasi.

---

[6] See Ellis (2000); Farrington, Deshingkar, Johnson and Start (2006)..

Table 1 *Distribution of households, by number of sources of income, Rewasi, 2009–10* (per cent)

Number of sources of income	Proportion of households
1	0.5
2	10.0
3	29.7
4	38.4
5	16.0
6	4.6
7	0.5
8	0.5
Total	100.0

Source: Survey data.

Table 2 *Income shares from agriculture and non-agriculture for poor and rich households, Rewasi, 2009–10*

Activity	Poorest 40%	Richest 10%
Agriculture	43	16
Non-agriculture	57	84

Source: Survey data.

Table 3 *Composition of household incomes of bottom 40 per cent and top 10 per cent households, Rewasi, 2009–10*

Activity	Bottom 40%	Top 10%
Self-employed in agriculture	36.5	16.2
Agricultural wage	6.5	0.0
Non-agricultural wage	17.7	1.2
Salary	10.2	4.4
Self-employed in non-agriculture	5.6	53.0
All other sources	23.4	25.2

Source: Survey data.

> For households in the lowest four deciles, incomes from self-employ-
> ment in agriculture, followed by non-agricultural wages, were the two
> main sources of income. For the richest households, self employment
> in non-agriculture was the major source of income. To put it differently,
> both rich and poor have multiple sources of income, but due to lack of
> resources for investment and appropriate education and skills, the poor
> are unable to invest in non-agricultural self-employment.
>
> *Source*: Bakshi (2015).

The incomes of households engaged in artisan work were very low. In 2009,
the average income of a household belonging to this class was Rs 25,374. It may
be noted that on account of low incomes from artisanal work, many workers
from these households had migrated to other cities to work in non-agricultural
occupations. In particular, men from the Kumawat (pot-maker) caste have
diversified into construction-related occupations. They migrated to work as
construction workers, masons, tile-layers, plumbers, etc. Only two households
continued to do pot-making. Similarly, some workers from Lohar (blacksmith)
households had specialised as welders.

Employment and Wages

Conditions of employment in rural India are characterised by low levels of
employment in terms of the days for which wage labourers find work (Dhar
2013a, 2013b; Ramachandran and Rawal 2010; Ramachandran, Swaminathan
and Rawal 2002; Ramachandran, Rawal and Swaminathan 2010; Rawal 2006).
The literature on gender disparities in employment shows that while men work
both within the village and outside, most rural women workers do not go out
of the village seeking work. This typically results in women working only in
agriculture (Dhar 2013b; Rawal 2006).

The conditions of employment in Rewasi broadly conform to these overall
patterns. It may be noted that the class of Hired workers was relatively small in
Rewasi, comprising thirty households or 18 per cent of all resident households.
Most of these households owned some land. However, given the small size
of their holdings and lack of irrigation, these lands had very little productive
potential. On average, there were 1.5 workers per household. Wage labour was

the primary means of livelihood for households classified as Hired workers. In addition to workers from this class, workers from middle and poor peasant classes as well as workers from households primarily dependent on artisanal work also participated in wage labour. Tables 3.49 to 3.52 show some features of employment of workers belonging to the class of Hired workers. The following features of employment are noteworthy.

First, the levels of labour absorption in agriculture, particularly in bad agricultural years like 2009–10, were low. Failure of the kharif crop in 2009–10 meant that very little labour was deployed in the kharif season. As discussed earlier, a large part of the land was left fallow in the rabi season in Rewasi. As a result, only 24 per cent of male casual workers reported working *only* in agriculture in the reference year. On the other hand, about 30 per cent of male casual workers worked in both agriculture and non-agricultural occupations, and another 28 per cent worked at only MGNREGS employment.

Secondly, for wage labourers, working in non-agricultural occupations was associated with migration. Travelling to the nearest city, Sikar, took more than an hour by public transport and casual workers could not afford to commute to Sikar in search of non-agricultural employment. There were no major non-agricultural enterprises in Rewasi. Activities related to construction of houses were the only source of non-agricultural casual employment within the village and in neighbouring habitations.

In Rewasi, in 2009–10, a male worker received an average of 105 days of wage employment and a female worker received 72 days of wage employment (Table 3.50). If the number of days of work received under the MGNREGS (Mahatma Gandhi National Rural Employment Guarantee Scheme) is excluded from the total number of days of employment, a male worker in Rewasi received only 84 days and a female worker merely 20 days of wage employment in the reference year.

Table 3.49 *Proportion of Hired workers employed in agricultural and non-agricultural wage work, by sex, Rewasi, 2009–10* (per cent)

	Only agriculture	Only non-agriculture	Both	Only MGNREGS
Male workers	24	18	30	28
Female workers	60	0	5	35
All workers	37	12	22	30

Source: Survey data.

Table 3.50 *Days of employment in agriculture and non-agricultural occupations, by sex, Hired worker class, Rewasi, 2009–10*

	Agriculture	MGNREGS	Other non-agricultural occupations	Total
Men	29	21	55	105
Women	20	52	–	72
Total	26	32	37	95

Note: Days of employment reported for MGNREGS refer to days for which payment was received and not days of actual work.
Source: Survey data.

Table 3.51 *Proportion of workers in the Hired worker class, by size-class of days of employment, Rewasi, 2009–10* (per cent)

Size-class of days of employment	Excluding MGNREGS	Including MGNREGS
1–30 days	50	30
31–60 days	15	20
61–90 days	7	8
91–120 days	12	10
121–150 days	5	8
151–180 days	2	10
> 180 days	10	13
All workers	100	100

Source: Survey data.

The distribution of workers by size-class of number of days of employment was highly skewed: 72 per cent of workers received employment for less than three months in a year, excluding the number of days of employment reported in MGNREGS job cards (Table 3.51). Further, 50 per cent of casual workers were employed for less than 30 days in 2009–10. At the other end of the distribution, only 10 per cent of workers received employment for more than six months. To put it differently, 91 per cent of all Hired workers obtained employment for less than half a year.

Table 3.52 shows that construction-related activities accounted for 69 per cent of days of non-agricultural work, and skilled work (for example, plumbers, electricians and masons) for about 17 per cent of days of non-agricultural work.

Table 3.52 *Share of different activities in total days of non-agricultural employment (excluding notional work under MGNREGS), Hired worker class, Rewasi, 2009–10* (per cent)

Type of work	Share (per cent)
Construction and related activities	69
Technicians (electricians, plumbers, welders, etc.)	17
Transport-related work	6
Loading/unloading	0
Shop attendants	1
Other	7
Total	100

Source: Survey data.

MGNREGS

In 2009–10, in Rewasi, no employment was generated under the Mahatma Gandhi National Rural Employment Guarantee Scheme (MGNREGS). Some workers were however paid for work, without actually having done any work. This notional non-agricultural employment was the main work that showed up in the work calendar of women workers as work in non-agricultural occupations. Only one woman worker from the class of Hired workers was engaged in non-agricultural employment (as a construction worker) other than under MGNREGS.

In the PARI survey year of 2010, a year of kharif crop failure, transfer payments were made to Hired workers under MGNREGS. The panchayat paid

Table 3.53 *Average number of days of wage employment obtained by Hired workers in agricultural and non-agricultural work, by sex, Rewasi, 2009–10* (8-hour days)

	Agricultural work	Non-agricultural work	
		MGNREGS*	Other
Male workers	29	21	55
Female workers	20	52	1
All workers	26	32	37

Note: *These are the average number of days of work for male, female, and all workers, for which they received payment from the panchayat.
Source: Survey data.

eighteen workers (eleven males and seven females) an average wage of Rs 100 per day. The hypothetical number of days of work (based on total wages received) ranged from 5 to 120, and amounted to 46 per cent of the total number of days of employment in non-agricultural tasks.

MGNREGS employment accounted for 46 per cent of non-agricultural employment obtained by Hired worker households. However, our data indicate that in Rewasi village, workers received wages for an average of thirty-two days per worker in the year; that is, this payment was more or less a transfer payment.

Migrant workers

The PARI survey showed that a very large number of workers migrated from Rewasi. A total of 145 migrant workers were reported in the survey (135 males and 10 females). The majority of migrant workers were males who left the village seeking employment. Around one-third of migrant men were engaged in non-agricultural activities other than construction and manufacturing, 13 per cent of male migrants were engaged in construction-related work and 19 per cent in manufacturing activities.

Migrant workers were employed in a variety of skilled technical occupations: as masons, tile layers, plumbers, electricians and drivers. They migrated to various cities across the country as well as to countries of West Asia (Middle East). International migrants typically went for a few months to a year, earned money and returned. Migrants to other cities in India often migrated for longer durations while visiting the village occasionally. They sent money to their families in Rewasi as well as brought money home when they came back.

International migrants constituted 24 per cent of all migrants; about 61 per cent were internal migrants who went to other States of India. The average age of a migrant worker in Rewasi was 31 years, and a migrant was more likely to be single as compared to a worker resident in the village. There was no big difference between the educational attainments of migrants and resident workers.

Migration in search of employment was a means to diversify household income. Young, unmarried men with little education and skills ventured out in search of employment, and were most likely to be engaged in non-agricultural activities. Construction and manufacturing were the two industries where a majority of migrant workers were employed. In Rewasi, migrants of the upper caste were over-represented in the migrant profile: 41 per cent of migrants belonged to the social group 'Others' (that is, not SC, ST or OBC) and 36 per cent belonged to OBCs. When the earnings of a migrant worker at the origin

Table 3.54 *Average daily wage earnings per male worker, Rewasi, 2010* (Rs)

Type of worker	Agriculture & related activities	Construction	Manufacturing
Male migrant worker	–	170	195
Male worker residing in village	150	152	150

Source: Survey data.

and destination were compared, the earnings of a migrant worker employed in the manufacturing sector were found to be almost 30 per cent higher than the corresponding non-agricultural wage in the village (Table 3.54).

RURAL CREDIT

Incidence and Burden of Debt

The incidence of indebtedness in Rewasi was extraordinarily high: 70 per cent of the households in the village were indebted at the time of the survey. The average amount of debt outstanding was also high, at around Rs 1.69 lakhs, and the debt to asset ratio averaged 18 per cent. The burden of debt as measured by the debt to asset ratio was higher for less wealthy households (with assets below the village average) as compared to more wealthy households. To put it differently, paying off outstanding debts would require 22 per cent of the assets of households with below-average assets.

Sources of Debt

Taking two broad sources of borrowing, namely formal and informal sources, as observed in other villages, it was found that there was a wide differential

Table 3.55 *Incidence and burden of debt by asset ownership, Rewasi, 2010*

	All households	Households with assets below average	Households with assets above average
Percentage of indebted households	70	72	66
Average amount of debt (Rs)	1,69,221	72,062	2,52,483
Debt–assets ratio (per cent)	17.9	22.2	15.6

Source: Survey data.

between the share of formal sources in total debt and in total number of loans. Formal sources accounted for 43 per cent of outstanding debts, but only 17 per cent of all loans outstanding. Within the formal sector, banks were the predominant source of credit in Rewasi (Table 3.56). The village was served by a commercial bank as well as a regional rural bank (RRB), and the residents had access to a cooperative bank as well.

In Rewasi, the informal sector was highly fragmented in nature (Table 3.56). There were landlords, small and medium peasants, traders, and various types of occasional lenders including salaried persons (such as professionals employed in the army and local schools) who catered to credit needs of the villagers. There was no major presence of professional moneylenders in the village. There was also no visible presence of self-help groups (SHGs) or micro-finance institutions (MFIs). There were, however, a few private finance companies, including Shriram Transport Finance, which lent to households in Rewasi.

The dependence on informal sources in the village was once again borne out

Table 3.56 *Distribution of amount of debt and number of loans by source, Rewasi, 2010*

Source	Amount of debt	Share in total amount	Number of loans	Share in total number of loans
Formal sources	1,61,48,302	43.0	67	16.6
Commercial banks	1,50,78,923	40.1	64	15.9
Cooperatives	10,69,379	2.9	3	0.7
Informal sources	2,14,18,840	57.0	336	83.4
Professional moneylenders	4,69,821	1.3	5	1.2
Salaried persons	11,72,820	3.1	31	7.7
Employers	1,61,200	0.4	1	0.3
Landlords	61,85,714	16.5	94	23.3
Small and medium peasants	15,76,946	4.2	62	15.4
Trader/other service provider	31,74,643	8.5	61	15.1
Private finance companies	45,27,825	12.0	7	1.7
Other and unspecified informal sources	31,52,690	8.4	35	8.7
Other occasional lenders	9,97,181	2.6	40	10.0
Total	3,75,67,142	100.0	403	100.0

Source: Survey data.

by the fact that 69 per cent of total indebted households borrowed exclusively from these sources and did not approach the formal sector at all for credit. By contrast, 18 per cent of indebted households met their credit needs only from formal sources of credit. The reliance on informal sources was more for asset-poor households. About 93 per cent of households having assets below the village average reported at least one loan from the informal sector. By contrast, only one-fourth of these households reported having accessed a loan from the formal sector. The situation was exactly the opposite for households having assets above the village average: three-fourths of these households reported at least one formal sector loan; however, about 65 per cent of these households approached the informal sector for a loan.

Across socio-economic classes, the share of formal sources in debt outstanding was the highest for landlord and rich peasant households. Interestingly, this amount accounted for a much smaller percentage of total loans taken by this class, indicating that access to formal credit was skewed within this class. The share of formal sources in debt outstanding and number of loans came down as we moved from landlord and rich peasant households to Hired worker households (Table 3.57).

Except for three socio-economic classes (namely landlords and the rural

Table 3.57 *Share of formal sources in debt outstanding and number of loans, by selected socio-economic classes, Rewasi, 2010*

Socio-economic class	Share of formal sources in	
	Debt outstanding	Number of loans
Landlords and rural rich	88.4	33.3
Peasants 1	65.5	50.0
Peasants 2	30.6	17.5
Peasants 3	37.1	20.7
Peasants 4	16.7	14.1
Hired worker households	4.7	3.4
Salaried person households	9.7	4.5
Business activity/self-employed	79.1	66.7
All households	43.0	16.6

Note: Households dependent on pensions and those engaged in artisanal work had no debt from the formal sector.
Source: Survey data.

Table 3.58 *Share of debt outstanding from informal sources, by type of source and socio-economic class, Rewasi, 2009–10 (per cent)*

Informal source	Socio-economic class								
	Landlords and rural rich	Peasant: 1	Peasant: 2	Peasant: 3	Peasant: 4	Hired workers	Artisan work and work at traditional caste calling	Business activity/self-employed	All households
Landlords/rich peasants	39.2	–	58.8	13.1	23.7	33.3	38.3	43.6	29.7
Friends and relatives	–	–	–	–	2.4	1.3	–	1.2	1.0
Employers	–	–	–	–	–	–	16.8	–	0.8
Private finance companies	–	–	–	67.3	13.3	3.3	–	–	21.1
Professional moneylenders	–	–	–	2.1	0.9	6.9	–	–	2.2
Salaried persons	17.2	100.0	15.5	1.8	0.5	7.2	17.1	7.3	5.9
Shop loans	–	–	–	0.9	1.4	1.5	0.5	2.0	1.2
Small and medium peasants	4.8	–	5.9	1.7	8.8	9.2	8.7	12.9	7.4
Traders/other service providers	38.9	–	19.8	9.6	25.3	8.7	17.0	9.4	14.8
Workers	–	–	–	–	0.8	0.3	–	5.8	1.3
Other and unspecified informal sources	–	–	–	3.5	22.9	28.3	1.5	17.7	14.6
All informal sources	100.0	100.0	100.0	100.0	100.0	100.0	100.0	100.0	100.0

Source: Survey data.

rich, households engaged in business activities, and Peasants 1 households), all others relied heavily on informal sources. Moreover, they relied on a variety of informal sources including landlords, small and medium peasants, salaried persons, private finance companies and professional moneylenders (Table 3.58).

Interest Rates on Debt

Interest rates at which loans were taken ranged from 0 to 48 per cent per annum, with a modal value of 24 per cent. The distribution of debt outstanding by interest rate mirrored the distribution by source of credit. Of the total amount of debt, 49 per cent was raised by households at rates ranging between 0 and 15 per cent per annum; this share closely corresponded to the share of formal sector in total debt (Table 3.59). Similarly, reflecting the dominance of the informal sector, about 73 per cent of the total loans were raised by households at rates ranging between 20 and 30 per cent per annum. Further, only 4 per cent of loans were raised at zero rate of interest, while nearly three-fourths of total loans were at rates exceeding 20 per cent per annum. Interest rates charged by different lenders are shown in Table 3.60.

The ratio of outstanding debt to total value of assets was almost 30 per cent for Hired worker households and artisanal households. As a result of relatively high interest rates on borrowing from the informal sector, the interest outstanding to assets ratio was also high, especially for Hired worker and artisan households.

Table 3.59 *Distribution of amount of debt and number of loans by interest rates, Rewasi, 2010*

Rate of interest	Amount of debt	Share in amount	Number of loans	Share in number of loans
0	2,68,600	0.7	17	4.2
0 < rate < 15	1,82,09,939	48.5	75	18.6
15 < rate < 20	32,33,938	8.6	11	2.7
20 < rate < 30	1,52,52,015	40.6	294	73.0
30 < rate < 40	2,56,400	0.7	5	1.2
40 < rate < 50	3,46,250	0.9	1	0.3
Total	3,75,67,142	100	403	100.0

Source: Survey data.

Table 3.60 *Mean and modal rates of interest by informal source, Rewasi, 2009–10* (per cent per annum)

Informal source	Mean	Mode
Emigrant workers	24	24
Friends and relatives	0	0
Landlords/rich peasants	23	24
Employers	24	24
Private finance companies	14	15
Professional moneylenders	24	24
Salaried persons	25	24
Shop loan	23	24
Small and medium peasants	23	24

Source: Survey data.

Table 3.61 *Debt and interest outstanding to assets ratio, by socio-economic class, Rewasi, 2010* (per cent)

Socio-economic class	Debt to asset ratio	Interest outstanding to asset ratio
Landlords and rural rich	20.3	0.8
Peasants 1	7.6	1.1
Peasants 2	19.9	3.8
Peasants 3	18.0	3.0
Peasants 4	21.3	5.5
Households in business activity/self-employed	2.2	0.2
Hired worker households	29.3	8.7
Artisan households engaged in work at traditional caste calling	28.5	7.4
Households relying on pension and handouts	7.7	2.2
Salaried person households	28.8	5.6
All classes	17.9	16.8

Source: Survey data.

Purposes of Debt

Our data suggest that the most frequently stated purpose for borrowing was for activities that were directly income-generating, particularly non-agricultural activities such as business and trade (Table 3.62). Not surprisingly, 79 per cent of borrowing from the formal sector was for directly productive activities. However, many households in Rewasi also approached informal lenders for credit to meet their production needs, probably because of the low level of formal sector development in the village. Of the total debt taken from informal sources, 37 per cent was for activities that were directly income-generating.

Table 3.62 *Distribution of amount of debt and number of loans by purpose, Rewasi, 2010*

Purpose	Amount of debt (Rs)	Share in total amount of debt (%)	Number of loans	Share in total number of loans (%)
Directly income-generating	2,07,26,575	55.2	124	30.8
Agriculture	47,34,816	12.6	54	13.4
Non-agriculture	1,59,91,759	42.6	70	17.4
Not directly income-generating	1,65,19,274	44.0	274	68.0
Ceremonial expenditure	45,56,719	12.1	74	18.4
Housing	40,19,539	10.7	60	14.9
Medical expenses	16,71,440	4.5	32	7.9
All other household expenses	62,71,576	16.7	108	26.8
Unspecified	3,21,293	0.9	5	1.2
Total	3,75,67,142	100.0	403	100.0

Source: Survey data.

ACCESS TO BASIC AMENITIES

Rewasi village comprises a main settlement and a number of satellite settlements called *dhani*s. About half the households live in the main settlement, while the rest live in the *dhani*s. Typically, a *dhani* is established by a household that builds a house on a part of its agricultural land. Over time, with the partitioning of households, these *dhani*s come to have multiple houses. Over the last two to three decades, a number of households in Rewasi, particularly from the Jat community, have moved from the main village settlement and built houses on their fields. Many of these families that lived in the fields had their ancestral homes, which were often owned jointly by several households in the present generation, in the main settlement. Some of these ancestral houses were abandoned; in some, a branch of the family continued to live.

If a household had a substantial amount of agricultural land – and the land had an electricity connection and a tubewell – there were distinct advantages of living on fields rather than in the main settlement. With an electricity-powered tubewell, the household got easy access to water. Also, the electricity connection could be used to power domestic equipment (though illegal, this was commonly done). In addition to better access to electricity and water, living on agricultural land facilitated better supervision of agriculture. Living on the fields made it easier for households to graze their animals on their fallows and to bring fodder for the animals. Households that lived in the *dhani*s could take their animals to the fields for direct manuring. It became easier to transport inputs and produce between home and the field.

The biggest *dhani* in Rewasi, set up by Chandraram Meena, had about twenty households in the survey year. The present heads of these households were third or fourth-generation descendants of Chandraram Meena. There were a number of single-household *dhani*s set up at different points of time over the last two decades or so.

Table 3.63 shows data on two indicators of adequacy of housing. The first is the quality of housing, based on materials used for construction of roof, walls

Table 3.63 *Proportion of households having houses with* pucca *roof, walls and floor and houses with two rooms and kitchen, by selected socio-economic classes, Rewasi, 2010* (per cent)

Socio-economic class	*Pucca* roof, walls and floor	Two or more rooms and kitchen
Landlords and rural rich	100	100
Peasants 1	100	79
Peasants 2	92	73
Peasants 3	90	79
Peasants 4	79	58
Hired workers	92	51
All households	88	67

Source: Survey data.

Table 3.64 *Proportion of households having houses with electricity, drinking water and toilets, by selected socio-economic classes, Rewasi, 2010* (per cent)

Socio-economic class	Electricity	Drinking water facility	Toilet
Landlords and rural rich	75	88	88
Peasants 1	71	93	8
Peasants 2	62	88	48
Peasants 3	53	80	46
Peasants 4	54	75	27
Hired workers	46	77	24
All households	54	81	36

Source: Survey data.

Table 3.65 *Proportion of households with fully* pucca *house, electricity connection, drinking water and toilets, by selected socio-economic classes, Rewasi, 2010* (per cent)

Socio-economic class	Per cent
Landlords and rural rich	63
Peasants 1	8
Peasants 2	28
Peasants 3	24
Peasants 4	16
Hired workers	19
All households	21

Source: Survey data.

and floor. In Rewasi, 88 per cent of households had houses with *pucca* roof, walls and floor. However, in terms of the second indicator of adequacy, there was a sharp drop in the proportion of households having houses with at least two rooms and a kitchen, as one moved from landlords and richer sections of the peasantry to poorer sections of the peasantry and Hired workers. While the houses of all landlord and rural rich households had at least two rooms and a kitchen, only 51 per cent of Hired workers had houses that met these criteria.

For other basic amenities, we examined the proportion of households across different socio-economic classes that had electricity, drinking water facility and toilets in their house (Table 3.64). The table shows that there was a substantial gap in the access of poor peasant and Hired worker households to these basic amenities. Of all Hired worker households, 46 per cent had electricity in their houses, 77 per cent had drinking water facility in their houses and only 24 per cent had a toilet. The availability of toilets was inadequate for all households except those belonging to landlords and rural rich.

Taking an integrated view of housing and going beyond the official discussion based on type of structure (*katcha/pucca*), we define an adequate house as one with a fully *pucca* structure – i.e. roof, walls and floor all made of *pucca* materials such as brick, cement, concrete, iron, stone, etc. – domestic electricity connection, drinking water within the house premises and a functional lavatory. We found that only one-fifth of all households in Rewasi had adequate housing as defined above. There was not much difference across different socio-economic classes (Table 3.65) except in the case of landlords and rural rich households, among whom 63 per cent had adequate housing.[7]

Rewasi belongs to the semi-arid region of Rajasthan, and although over 96 per cent of households in the village owned some land, given very limited access to irrigation, the productivity of land was very low. In Rewasi, ownership of tubewells and other sources of irrigation was critical for agricultural production. Furthermore, the reference year of our survey, 2009–10, was a year of low rainfall and widespread crop failure in the kharif season. As a result, agricultural incomes were very low that year. However, as our data on costs and incomes from cultivation show, the economic impact of drought was differential across classes. With better access to irrigation and capital, landlords and richer sections of the peasantry were better able to withstand drought-like conditions and contain their losses. On the other hand, poor peasants and cultivating households from the class of Hired workers incurred substantial losses as a result of drought.

The distribution of land in Rewasi was not as unequal as in many irrigated villages (such as 25 F Gulabewala). The proportion of households with no agricultural land was small, only 4 per cent. Around 53 per cent of households owned and operated small holdings, that is, below 5 acres. Nevertheless, the distribution of non-land assets was highly unequal, resulting in high overall

---

[7] The inadequacy of housing among Peasants 1 households was because their houses, which were located on the fields, lacked toilets.

wealth inequality. Landlords and rural rich households constituted 4 per cent of all households and owned 20 per cent of all assets. Hired workers constituted 18 per cent of all households and owned 7 per cent of all assets.

In the survey year, incomes from agriculture were meagre and constituted a relatively small share of total household income for most households. While richer sections of the village derived substantial incomes from businesses and salaried jobs, poor peasants and Hired workers depended substantively on wage labour. Availability of wage employment within the village was limited, and a number of workers from Rewasi migrated to different parts of India as well as to other countries, in particular to West Asia. A majority of migrants from Rewasi worked in skilled occupations. More than one-half of households surveyed in the village received remittances in the reference year, averaging Rs 31,000 per household. Another important source of income was from animal husbandry. The majority of households owned animals; 94 per cent of households owned goats. Animal resources were thus an important means to sustain incomes and nutrition in bad agricultural years.

In respect of education, both of children and adults, the situation in Rewasi was far from satisfactory. Attendance rates fell sharply, especially for girls, after the age of 14. Child labour was prevalent in the village. There was a huge gap, of 30 percentage points, between the literacy levels of men and women in the village. For the large majority, conditions of housing and availability of basic amenities were highly inadequate.

In this chapter, we have used the lens of socio-economic classes to study various aspects of the economy of Rewasi village, including crop production and income from other sources, ownership and control of land and other assets, aspects of employment, and access to credit. We argue that location in the class hierarchy, particularly for those at the two ends, is critical for understanding economic and non-economic aspects of living standards.

APPENDIX 1
JAGIRDARI SYSTEM IN SHEKHAWATI

Vikas Rawal

The *jagirdari* system originated in Rajputana in the medieval period as a system of military control and administration of the Rajput states. By the early twentieth century, the *jagirdari* system of Jaipur State, of which Shekhawati was a part, had evolved into an extremely complex system of land administration. Land was divided between *jagir* (or *thikana*) and *khalsa* lands. *Jagirs* were awarded to Rajput military chiefs, who administered it relatively autonomously, in return for payment of revenue and provision of military services to the State of Jaipur.[8] Jaipur principality and big *jagirdars* kept some land directly under their control; they determined the rate of revenue on these lands and made their collections through revenue collectors. These were called *khalsa* lands. Jaipur State had no *khalsa* land of its own in Shekhawati, and all the land was under the control of different *jagirdars*. Big *jagirdars* like Rao Raja of Sikar had considerable *khalsa* lands on which they determined rates of revenue, as well as *jagir* land, which was in turn awarded to smaller *jagirdars*. Sub-infeudation was a fundamental feature of the *jagirdari* system in Jaipur State and it was common for *jagirdars* to award different parts of the *jagir* to smaller *jagirdars* (Stern 1988).

There were many categories of *jagirdars* with variations in respect of the size of land, on account of whether the award had been made by the State or by a superior *jagirdar*, and on account of the types of obligations towards the superior authority. There were several categories of small *jagirdars*: at the bottom of the ladder were the *bhumia jagirdars* who did not have any military capabilities and merely provided revenue to the superior *jagirdars* or to the Rajput crown (Tod 1920; Sisson 1971; Stern 1988; Sharma 1992).

About half of the land in Sikar was the *jagir* of Rao Raja of Sikar (that is, on this land revenue was paid by the peasants directly to Rao Raja), while the rest was awarded to smaller *jagirdars* who collected revenue from the peasants (Pande 1982; Ram 1986). All *jagir* holders in Shekhawati belonged to different clans of the Rajput caste.

---

[8] The need for Jaipur State to mobilise military services through *jagirdars* declined after the State signed a treaty of subordinate domination with the British in 1818. After this treaty, external affairs became a responsibility of the British. However, the State still depended upon *jagirdars* to provide military forces for managing its internal affairs.

Sikar was the biggest *thikana* under Jaipur principality. It covered about 3.7 lakh hectares (1,455 square miles) of land and consisted of 436 villages (Tod 1920; Ram 1986). According to accounts provided by James Tod for the early nineteenth century, Sikar *thikana* accounted for about 35 per cent of total revenues collected by Jaipur principality from various *jagir*s (Tod 1920). Land was cultivated by tenants-at-will who could be alienated by the *jagirdar*s unilaterally and arbitrarily. Of various peasant castes that worked as tenants, Jats were the most numerous and cultivated the largest share of land. According to 1931 Census data, Jats accounted for 25.7 per cent of the population and cultivated (as tenants) 56.7 per cent of the agricultural land in Sikar *thikana*.[9]

In the early twentieth century, the conditions of peasants in Sikar *thikana*, and in Jaipur State in general, were characterised by a very high burden of land revenue and other taxes imposed by the *jagirdar*s. The rates of land revenue were determined arbitrarily and were changed at will by the *jagirdar*s. Jaipur State and the big *jagirdar*s auctioned the right of revenue collection on their *khalsa* lands to the highest bidder. There were no definite laws regarding land revenue and no official records were maintained. As explained by Sharma (1990 and 1992), under the prevalent practice, revenue officers of the *thikana,* who were called *latara*, made a visual assessment (*kunt*) of the standing crops of the peasants. The share of land revenue was determined on the basis of this visual estimate. The rate of land revenue was usually fixed as half of the estimated production, but could be set at a higher level arbitrarily. The visual estimate was typically much higher than the actual production and available records suggest that in some cases, the land revenue even exceeded actual production. Among other reasons, rates of land revenue were increased beyond 50 per cent to meet the requirements of *jagirdar*s on account of war, birth, death and marriage in their families, and for coronation ceremonies of inheritors.

Not only were peasants charged very high land revenue, they also had to pay a very large number of other taxes (*lag*), which together were even higher in value than the land revenue. Taxes were imposed for keeping animals, for using natural resources like firewood from trees, for using water for animals and irrigation, and for use of pastures and wild bushes. Taxes (*zakat*) were imposed on goods transported from one village to another and from one *thikana* to another. In addition, peasants had to provide various kinds of unpaid labour services (*bag*) as well as meet other demands (for example, providing

---

[9] Census of India, 1931 cited in Stern (1988), Ram (1986) and Sharma (1992).

camels to *jagirdars*). The peasant castes, including Jats, were subject to various civic restrictions: for example, they were not allowed to wear gold ornaments, ride horses and elephants, and, in some cases, not even allowed to live in *pucca* houses (Sharma 1990 and 1992).

Peasant Struggles in Shekhawati

Major struggles of peasants against the *jagirdari* system started in Sikar in the 1920s. Historians of these peasant struggles have identified several factors that inspired the Jat peasantry in Shekhawati to struggle against *jagirdari* oppression. The Arya Samaj, which had considerable influence among the Jat peasantry, was instrumental in motivating peasants to oppose the excesses of *jagirdars* (Ram 1986). Peasant movements elsewhere in Rajasthan, most notably the Bijolia peasant struggle, and other contemporary peasant struggles in the country were also directly influential (Ram 1986; Pande 1986; Sharma 1990).[10] Jats in areas under the control of the British had acquired considerable political and economic power. Jat leaders from these areas were actively involved in organising Shekhawati's Jats to protest against the excesses of Rajput *jagirdars* (Stern 1988; Sharma 1992). Sharma (1992) notes the influence of international developments – in particular of peasants from Shekhawati who joined the British army and participated in the First World War, and of the Russian revolution – on leaders of the Bijolia and Shekhawati peasant struggles.

Peasant struggles in Shekhwati originated in 1922 as protests against arbitrary increases in demands of land revenue by the Rao Raja (*thikanedar*) of Sikar, in a year that had seen widespread drought and crop failure. Sharma (1992) has identified three phases in the peasant struggles of Shekhawati between the 1920s and 1950s, when the *jagirdari* system was abolished.

Phase I: Struggles between 1922 and 1930

The first phase, from 1922 to about 1930, consisted of incipient attempts to demand relief against the excesses of the *jagirdars*, in particular Rao Raja of Sikar. During this phase, representatives of peasants took advantage of contradictions between the *jagirdars* and Jaipur State, which was then directly under British administration, and appealed to the State and the British authori-

---

[10] Harlal Singh, a prominant Jat leader from Shekhawati, met Bijay Singh Pathik and Baba Sitaram Das, the most important leaders of the Bijolia movement, in 1921 (Ram 1986). Ram Narain Chaudhary, another leader of the Bijolia movement, was directly involved in the initial efforts at building the peasant movement in Shekhawati (Sharma 1990).

ties against the excesses of Rao Raja. The establishment of the Shekhawati Jat Sabha in 1925, as an arm of the All-India Jat Mahasabha, provided the organisational basis for the peasant movements in this phase.[11] Major success of the peasant movement in this phase included the reversal of increases in land revenue as a result of intervention by the Jaipur State. This was a major achievement that encouraged peasants to further intensify their struggles. It is also noteworthy because, as a result of the struggles of peasants, Jaipur State was forced to intervene in matters that were till then considered autonomous domains of the *jagirdars*. However, these achievements only provided them temporary relief, and the larger demands of peasants – in respect of abolition of labour services, regulation of other taxes, civic rights, and for improvements of facilities for health and education – remained unmet.

Phase II: 1930 through 1938

According to Sharma (1992), the second phase, from 1930 through 1938, was a period of organisational consolidation of the Shekhawati peasant movement. Kisan Jat Panchayats and Kisan Sabhas were organised during these period. The Shekhawati Kisan Sabha, headed by Tarakeshwar Sharma, was formed with the support of Socialists within the Congress. During this phase of the Shekhawati peasant movement, lines of struggles were more sharply drawn between Jat tenants and *jagirdars*. A number of violent incidents took place between Jat peasants and Rajput *jagirdars*, and the strength of the peasants grew (Sisson 1971; Sharma 1992). In August 1934, under pressure from the British, Rao Raja of Sikar agreed to a number of demands of the peasants including waiver of taxes, permission to use pasture-land for grazing, and abolition of *bag* (unpaid labour services). However, the agreement was not implemented and the peasants further intensified their struggle.

Phase III: 1938 through 1940s

The third phase, from 1938 until end of 1940s, was a period in which the Indian National Congress, through the Jaipur State Praja Mandal, became involved in issues of the peasantry in Shekhawati. The involvement, and coming to dominance, of the Praja Mandal critically determined the future course of the peasant movement and eventual abolition of the *jagirdari* system in the

---

[11] The All-India Jat Mahasabha was closely related to the Arya Samaj. Links with the All-India Jat Mahasabha also provided support of Jat peasant leaders from British areas, most importantly Punjab (Ram 1986; Sharma 1992).

early 1950s. Until 1938, the Congress leadership had been indifferent, and had openly dissociated itself from peasant struggles in Rajasthan. The Praja Mandal, which was re-established in 1938, was primarily urban-based, and was led by the rich Marwari Bania community and Brahmans.[12] While the Praja Mandal leadership realised the importance of coopting the mature peasant movement of Shekhawati for expanding the political influence of the Praja Mandal in the region, sections of Kisan Panchayats and Kisan Sabhas were opposed to the peasant movement becoming a part of the Praja Mandal (Sisson 1971; Pande 1982). The Shekhawati Kisan Sabha continued to function independently. In 1938–39, the Kisan Sabha faced repression from the Jaipur State, and most of its leaders were either imprisoned or forced to leave Shekhawat (Pande 1982).

In 1938, Jaipur State forcibly took over the administration of Sikar *thikana* and sent Rao Raja Kalyan Singh into exile. Following this, land settlement was done in the *khalsa* lands that were earlier under the direct administration of Rao Raja. However, despite a decline in powers of smaller *jagirdar*s, Jaipur State and the British could not implement land settlement in *jagir* areas. In this phase, initially, both Jaipur State and the *thikanedar*s tried to get the support of the peasants by offering them concessions. However, with intensification of the Quit India movement, the peasant movement came under the broad leadership of the Praja Mandal, and Jaipur State and the British tried to repress the movement (Sharma 1992).

Peasant struggles in Shekhawati throughout these three phases were led by peasants belonging to the Jat caste. Caste organisations of Jats – the Shekhawati Jat Sabha in the 1920s, and Shekhawati Jat Kisan Panchayat – were in the forefront of these struggles through the 1930s and 1940s. Although not as organised as the Jats and not as large a group numerically, Brahmans were allies of Jats in these struggles. Brahmans enjoyed high caste status and social position, but they were economically poor. A number of leaders of the movement, of whom the most prominent was Tarakeshwar Sharma, were Brahmans.

The Marwari trader community, although wealthy, had no political position in Jaipur and did not have civic rights comparable to the ruling Rajputs. They had been influenced by the Congress, and had organised non-cooperation and *swadeshi* movements in Shekhawati since 1921. While Marwari traders-cum-moneylenders were themselves a parasitic class and Jat peasants were wary of them, the Marwari community tacitly supported struggles against Rajput *jagirdar*s

---

[12] Jamnalal Bajaj and G.D. Birla were in the leadership of the Praja Mandal.

by providing funds and facilitating contacts with the British (Sharma 1990).

There had been a few attempts at organising joint struggles of peasants from other castes, but these were not successful. In the late 1920s, leaders of the All India Jat Mahasabha formed the Ahir Jat Gujjar and Rajput Sabha in order to bring all peasant castes together. However, the Jats of Shekhawati left this organisation in 1929 to organise their movement separately. There was an uprising of Bairwa (Chamar) peasants in Unaira *thikana* in 1946. The All India State People Bairwa Mahasabha provided leadership to an independent movement of Bairwa peasants in Unaira between 1946 and 1949, a period in which Jat peasant movements merged into the Praja Mandal (Sharma 1990). Sisson (1966) notes that there was some participation of Sirvi and Vishnoi untouchable castes in Kisan Sabhas in Shekhawati in the late 1940s.

Abolition of Jagirdari System and Emergence of a New Land Structure

The most important piece of legislation for abolition of the *jagirdari* system, the Rajasthan Land Reforms and Resumption of Jagir Act, was adopted in 1952. Iyer (1995) has provided a summary of the legislative process of abolition of *jagirdari* in Rajasthan. As of 16 December 1957, the government resumed all rights on *jagir* lands. However, *khalsa* lands, orchards, non-agricultural lands, wells and buildings continued to belong to the *jagirdars*. *Jagirdars* were given compensation equivalent to seven times the net income from land, which was assessed at 30 per cent of the value of produce (Rudolph and Rudolph 2011). On erstwhile *jagir* lands, ownership (*khatedari*) rights were provided to those who were until then recognised only as tenants. In Rajasthan as a whole, a total of 200 lakh hectares of *jagir* land were resumed under the Jagirdari Abolition Act (Iyer 1995). Given the strength of the peasant movement in Sikar, the Jagirdari Abolition Act was implemented very successfully in Sikar.

According to the account provided by Rudolph and Rudolph (2011), big *jagirdars* of Rajasthan, who had substantial *khalsa* lands that were exempted from resumption under the Jagirdari Abolition Act, formed an association, the Kshatriya Mahasabha, and negotiated through legal and political means for higher compensation for their *jagir* lands. On the other hand, most small *jagirdars* had no *khalsa* land. Between 1943 and 1946, organisations of small *jagirdars* demanded that a part of their *jagir* lands be treated as *khalsa* land (Ram 1986). In the 1950s, small *jagirdars* formed a separate association, the Bhuswami Sangh, to struggle for exemption of small *jagirs* from resumption under the

Act.[13] However, as a result of the political strength of the Jat peasantry, the Bhuswami Sangh did not succeed in getting its demands accepted despite violent struggles in the early 1950s (Rudolph and Rudolph 2011). In Shekhawati, where all land was classified as *jagir* land, this had major implications.

Large Rajput *jagirdar*s in other parts of Rajasthan obtained substantial compensation on account of resumption of *jagir*s and had *khalsa* lands left for themselves. These families joined the Congress Party and continued to wield considerable social and political power in Rajasthan (Rudolph and Rudolph 2011).

In contrast, given that almost all land in Sikar was classified as *jagir* land, *jagirdar*s of Sikar lost most of their land and became impoverished. On the other hand, tenant peasants, who had faced the worst forms of social oppression at the hands of Rajput *jagirdar*s, acquired ownership (*khatedari*) rights over lands they had cultivated as tenants. Of the various castes, Jats had been the biggest tenants and were the most organised. They were thus the biggest beneficiaries of *jagirdari* abolition, which clearly turned upside down the relative economic positions of Jat peasants and Rajputs. In this respect, the experience of *jagirdari* abolition in Sikar was unique.

As in most of India, land ceiling and land redistribution were not implemented seriously in Rajasthan. Land reform laws were marred by serious loopholes, which were used by large landowners to evade ceilings (Iyer 1996b). Land ceilings were introduced in Rajasthan in 1960 through a provision of the Rajasthan Tenancy Act, 1955.[14] Given vast variations in the quality of land in Rajasthan, the ceilings defined under the Rajasthan Tenancy Act ranged from 22 acres to 336 acres per family (Government of India 1966). These ceilings could be relaxed for families with more than five members (Iyer 1995). There was a gap of three years between the enactment of the provision of land ceiling and formulation of the rules (Government of India 1966). Such a prolonged delay only helped to conceal ceiling surplus land through *benami* transfers. Given the vast variation in applicable ceilings, various kinds of relaxations that were allowed and lack of political support for implementation of the programme, very little progress was made in implementing land ceiling. Using data for

---

[13] The *jagirdari* system in Rajasthan followed strict rules of primogeniture and *jagir*s were inherited by the eldest son in the family. Younger sons of big *jagirdar*s served in courts and as managers of estates. With the abolition of *jagirdari*, this section of Rajputs also faced economic ruin and joined small *jagirdar*s in the Bhuswami Sangh (Rudolph and Rudolph 2011).

[14] A separate Rajasthan Imposition of Ceiling on Agricultural Holdings Act was enacted in 1973.

1970–71, Bandyopadhyay (1986) estimated ceiling-surplus land in Rajasthan to be about 40 lakh hectares. In contrast, until 2007, only about 2.3 lakh hectares of ceiling surplus land had been taken possession of (Government of India 2008). This was only about 1 per cent of cultivable land in the State. Tenancy laws in Rajasthan do not restrict leasing of land and merely specify statutory rates of rent that can be charged. Even these provisions for regulating terms of tenancy are applicable to only those tenants and sub-tenants who have a legally valid contract between lessor and lessee (Srinivas 1995). This obviously excludes a vast majority of tenancy contracts that remain informal and oral.

The historical evidence reviewed here shows that the emergence of economically and politically dominant landlords from among Jat and, to a smaller extent, Brahman castes in Shekhawati is a relatively recent phenomenon. Peasant struggles in the first half of the twentieth century broke open the shackles of the *jagirdari* system. Abolition of *jagirdari* brought about a fundamental change in the structure of control over land in Shekhawati, with tenants-at-will getting ownership rights over land. In Sikar, struggles by the peasantry and *jagirdari* abolition effectively ended the domination of Rajputs over land. The contemporary agrarian structure seen in Rewasi suggests that, with the erosion of control of former *jagirdars* over land, in the post-*jagirdari* abolition period, a few households belonging to Jat and Brahman castes in the village acquired substantial economic and political power, to emerge as new landlords.

4

Conclusion

In this study, we have examined the socio-economic features of two villages in Rajasthan, 25 F Gulabewala in Sri Ganganagar district and Rewasi in Sikar district, based on detailed village census surveys. These two villages and a third village, Dungariya in Udaipur district, were surveyed as part of the Project on Agrarian Relations in India (PARI). The three study villages are situated in three different agro-climatic regions of Rajasthan, and were selected to broadly represent the social and economic conditions of the respective regions. Of the three villages, 25 F Gulabewala and Dungariya were surveyed in 2007, and Rewasi was surveyed in 2010. In the previous two chapters, we have elaborated on the agrarian economy of 25 F Gulabewala and Rewasi. A detailed analysis of agrarian conditions in Dungariya can be found in Ramachandran (2010).

Rajasthan is divided into ten agro-climatic zones. In a State with such varying agro-ecological conditions, a study of three villages cannot capture the diversity of agrarian production conditions. Nevertheless, the rich data available on these three villages does give us a glimpse into the conditions of agricultural production and agrarian relations in Rajasthan.

Socio-Economic Class and Caste

In this book, as in other studies of PARI villages, households are stratified by the socio-economic class to which they belong. The analysis of the villages is thus undertaken from a class perspective, taking into account also the position of households in the caste hierarchies of the study villages. The exact categorisation may vary from village to village but is broadly based on three variables: the level and composition of incomes, labour deployment on land and in non-farm activities, and ownership of means of production.

Class structure in 25 F Gulabewala was characterised by clear and sharp differentiation between capitalist farmers, on the one hand, and the large majority of households of landless manual workers, on the other. In this village, paradoxically, development of capitalism in agriculture took place alongside the persistence of unfree labour relations, and was characterised by a near-perfect correlation between class structure and caste hierarchy.

In Rewasi, landlords and rural rich were at the top of the class hierarchy, followed by four categories of peasants. A relatively small proportion of households were of landless hired workers. Further, 9 per cent of the households were primarily dependent on salaried jobs, non-agricultural businesses or transfer payments (mainly remittances and pensions). In Rewasi, both poor peasants and hired workers participated in wage-based employment. Class and caste structure in contemporary Rewasi bears a marked influence of peasant struggles of the early twentieth century that culminated in the abolition of the *jagirdari* system. Rajputs occupied the dominant position and comprised a parasitic class until the time of abolition of *jagirdari*. Now, they are impoverished, and belong to the class of middle and poor peasants. On the other hand, Jats, formerly an oppressed caste of poor tenants who emerged as victors in the struggle against Rajput *jagirdar*s, occupy a dominant position in contemporary Rewasi. There are also some Brahman households in the category of landlords and rural rich, although historically Brahmans in Rewasi were not economically well off and had joined the Jats in the struggle against Rajput *jagirdar*s.

In contrast to 25 F Gulabewala and Rewasi, Dungariya is a tribal village with no landlords or big capitalist farmers. Most households in this village had some forest land to cultivate, held by them 'in owner-like possession, but *without legal title*' (emphasis in original). Some key observations made by Ramachandran (2010) on class relations in Dungariya are as follows:

> There is no landlord in the village, nor are there landlords outside the village who own land here.
>
> Inequality in the distribution of household land holdings in the village is lower than in other villages we have studied as part of the Project on Agrarian Relations in India (PARI).
>
> Differentiation among the peasantry is not absent in Dungariya. With irrigation

and the entry of the cash economy in agriculture, differentiation has begun in the village. Nevertheless, differentiation is not characterised primarily by differences in the *extent* of ownership holdings of land. Further, the nature of differentiation is not such as to make the resolution of contradictions between classes *within* the village an immediate political task.

Land and Wealth Inequality

Patterns of ownership of land and other assets closely follow the hierarchy of socioeconomic classes. In 25 F Gulabewala, a village with an exceptionally high level of inequality, the top 10 per cent of households (when ranked by extent of land owned) held 61 per cent of land, while the lowest 60 per cent of households owned less than 1 per cent of the total land. The top three classes – landlords and/or big capitalist farmers 1 and 2, and Farmers 1 – accounted for 21 per cent of households but owned 88 per cent of total wealth.

Inequality in ownership of land and assets was also high in Rewasi although only 4 per cent of households were landless. Economic inequality in Rewasi arose from the unequal distribution of irrigated land and means of production related to non-agricultural businesses. The top three classes in Rewasi (landlords and the rural rich, Peasants 1 and 2) comprised 21 per cent of all households, and cultivated 60 per cent of irrigated land in the kharif season and 57 per cent of irrigated land in the rabi season. Our study showed that the top 10 per cent of households (when ranked by total assets) owned 38 per cent of total wealth, while the bottom 50 per cent of households owned 19 per cent of total wealth of residents of the village.

In contrast, Dungariya was a village where most households lacked assets with any market value. This is how Ramachandran (2010) described the extreme asset poverty of Dungariya:

> Other than in three households – that of the flour miller, the small shopkeeper and the former public-works contractor and jeep-owner – assets were few and of low value.
>
> The most important household assets were essentially non-tradable commodities: agricultural land, huts and livestock-sheds. The walls of most huts were of wood and mud, mud and stone or mud and thatch. Only three households had any cement in their walls. All but ten households had earthen floors.

Agricultural Production and Crop Incomes

The three villages differ significantly in terms of the development of productive forces in agriculture.

Farming in 25 F Gulabewala represented relatively large-scale agriculture: the average size of land operated per household was 39 acres; farming practices were capital-intensive, with farmers owning a large stock of machinery. With input-intensive agriculture, and the application of high-yielding varieties, fertilizers and irrigation, crop yields were much higher than the averages for Rajasthan and India. A major constraint on the growth of productive forces was irrigation. Although cultivation of cotton in the kharif season yielded substantial net returns, in 2007–08, a large amount of land was left fallow in the kharif season on account of lack of availability of irrigation water. In recent years, the gap between demand and supply of water seems to have been eased to some extent with the spread of cluster bean cultivation, in response to a steep rise in prices of cluster beans.

Agricultural production in Rewasi was severely constrained by lack of access to irrigation. Cultivation in the kharif season was monsoon-dependent. In the rabi season, when rains were scarce, more than half of the operational holdings were left fallow. Ownership of tubewells and irrigation wells, which lay disproportionately in the hands of the rich, was crucial for agriculture in the village. Rewasi was surveyed in a year of low rainfall and widespread crop failures occurred in the kharif season with almost total failure of the pearl millet crop. As a result, agricultural incomes in the survey year were very low, constituting only 11 per cent of the total income of all households. However, the economic impact of drought was different across classes. Landlords and richer sections of the peasantry, who had access to irrigation and capital, were better able to contain their losses. On the other hand, poor peasants and cultivating households from the class of hired manual workers incurred substantial losses as a result of the drought.

Agriculture in Dungariya was characterised by an extremely low level of development of productive forces. As Ramachandran (2010) observed:

> A consequence of the relatively low levels of technological change has been low levels of production and productivity. Of 129 plots on which maize was grown in 2006–07, the crop failed entirely on 20 plots, and the average production on the other plots appears to have been about 420 kg per hectare. Wheat was grown on 81 plots that year, and average yields were about 1.4 tonnes per hectare.

Biological inputs. Most households used chemical fertilizers, but in small quantities, the peak being in the region of 100 kg per acre, and some as low as 10 kg. All households used home-produced seeds. No seeds were bought from the market in the reference year.

Implements and machinery. The most important implements used in the village come directly from the forest – every year or two, peasants make ploughs and levellers from wood they cut down from the forest.

Only six households used machinery for field preparation (including ploughing) the whole year, though most wheat-growers hired tractors to thresh wheat.

Draught animals are of a local long-horned variety. Low production levels mean low fodder production, and consequently, weak cattle.

Metal implements and shallow metal basins are often the only purchased items that households owned in the broad categories of means and implements of production.

Access to Credit

Rajasthan is a relatively under-banked State, with per capita bank credit being roughly half the average for the country as a whole. Of the three study villages, access to bank credit was highest in 25 F Gulabewala, but this was largely restricted to landowning Jat Sikh households. Households in Rewasi had extraordinarily high levels of indebtedness: about 70 per cent households were indebted, but less than half the outstanding debt (43 per cent) was from formal-sector sources. There were, of course, differences across socioeconomic classes: 88 per cent of the outstanding credit of landlords and 5 per cent of the outstanding credit of hired worker households came from formal-sector sources. In Dungariya village, not one household had a loan outstanding from any formal source of credit (bank or cooperative).

Household Incomes

In both 25 F Gulabewala and Rewasi, income inequality was high and delineated along class lines.

In 25 F Gulabewala, the class of Landlords and/or big capitalist farmers 1 accounted for 3 per cent of households and 43 per cent of total household income. Their average income was over Rs 20 lakhs per annum, eighty times that of an average manual worker household. Manual worker households comprised 56 per cent of all households and their income was only 9 per cent of total household income. Income inequality in 25 F Gulabewala was directly related to extremely unequal distribution of land. With high levels of yields and large size of landholdings, households belonging to Landlord and/or big capitalist farmer classes obtained very substantial incomes from agriculture. They also invested surpluses from agriculture into other businesses, which added to their incomes. On the other hand, given the limited availability of non-agricultural employment, low wages and unfree working conditions in agriculture, manual worker households received very low incomes. Of all the PARI village studies thus far, income inequality, as measured by the Gini coefficient, was highest in Gulabewala village.

In Rewasi, surveyed in a drought year, richer sections of the village derived substantial incomes from businesses and salaried jobs. Landlords and the rural rich accounted for only 4 per cent of households but 21 per cent of total household income. Given their marginal landholdings with no access to irrigation, poor peasants and hired workers were engaged in a range of non-agricultural occupations. Diversification of incomes was a striking feature of households in Rewasi. Livestock also played a very important role in the economy of households in Rewasi. In particular, ownership of goats provided a cushion against drought and was crucial for the food security of households. While maintenance of buffaloes and cows required land and water to grow fodder, goats survive on leaves from trees and shrubs that are available even in periods of drought. Building a stock of goats in normal agricultural years and selling some of them in a drought year was a common practice among poorer households in Rewasi.

While quantification of incomes was very difficult in Dungariya on account of limited participation in markets, Ramachandran (2010) noted that

> in any case, incomes were very low. Most households earned only about Rs 100 to Rs 120 per person per month (excluding forest produce). Of this, 60 per cent and more came from public works, particularly road building, and earnings from wages earned through temporary migration to the cotton fields and construction sites of Gujarat.

Wage Employment

Severe underemployment among manual workers was common to all three villages. In 25 F Gulabewala, on average, a male casual worker was employed for 141 days in a year and a female casual worker for 67 days. In Rewasi, an average male worker received wage employment for only 84 days in a year and an average female worker for 20 days in a year. In Dungariya, public works and cotton picking in Gujarat were the only sources of wage employment.

An important aspect of the agrarian economy of 25 F Gulabewala was that manual workers had very little access to non-agricultural employment. They worked primarily in agriculture, either as casual workers or as long-term workers. In contrast, a number of male workers from Rewasi migrated to different parts of India as well as to countries of West Asia. A majority of migrants from Rewasi worked in skilled occupations. Income from non-agricultural work located outside the village – received by households as direct earnings of household members or as remittances from other family members who had left these households on account of migration for work – accounted for a major share of income of manual worker and poor peasant households.

Rajasthan has been a high-achievement State in respect of the distribution of job cards and provision of employment under the National Rural Employment Guarantee Scheme (NREGS). In 2009–10, 71 per cent of rural households had job cards, and 62 per cent of rural households obtained work under NREGS for an average of 37 days per worker (Usami and Ramakumar, 2012). In Rewasi, we found that no employment was generated, but payments were received by job card holders equivalent to wages for 32 days per worker. In other words, NREGS payments took the form of transfer payments rather than wages. The situation was very different in Dungariya.

For workers of Dungariya, NREGS was an important source of employment. Ramachandran (2010) notes, 'for all the inadequacies of the wage and the drudgery involved, however, NREGS had become the single largest source of annual earnings for many households, a last barrier against complete disaster'. Also, 'large numbers of workers migrated to Gujarat to work at construction sites or in cotton fields. Cotton-pickers received Rs 40 a day with a portion of cooked vegetable or Rs 35 if they opted to take dal and roti as well.' In both 25 F Gulabewala and Rewasi, women were wage workers in agriculture and did not seek employment outside the village.

Education

Educational attainments were nothing to write home about in any of the three villages. In 25 F Gulabewala, the educational divide was along class and caste lines, with very poor attainments among Dalit manual worker households.

Median years of schooling for both adult men and women in Dalit manual worker households were zero. About half the children in the age-group 11 to 14 years from manual worker households did not attend school; many of these children were engaged in work. In Rewasi, a very visible divide is that between men and women. The literacy rate for women was only 46 per cent, while 76 per cent of men aged 7 years and above were literate. In Dungariya, deprivation in terms of the access to education was appalling (Ramachandran 2010). Of all Scheduled Tribe persons aged 7 years and above, only 18 per cent – 26 per cent of men and 9 per cent of women – were literate; and of all tribal children in the age-group 6 to 12 years, only 29 per cent – 38 per cent of boys and 20 per cent of girls – were attending school.

Access to Basic Amenities

The general level of access to basic amenities was extremely poor. Using a simple measure of adequate housing, namely, a house with roof, walls and floor made of *pucca* materials, two rooms, a toilet, electricity, and a source of water within or just outside the premises, the majority of households lived in inadequate houses. In 25 F Gulabewala, in aggregate, 32 per cent of households lived in houses that met all five criteria, but a staggering 97 per cent of Dalit households lived in houses that did not meet our criteria of adequate housing. In Rewasi, 63 per cent of households among landlords and the rural rich lived in houses that met these criteria, but the proportion was only 19 per cent among hired worker households. No house in Dungariya met our standards of an adequate house.

In this book, we have examined a range of variables for two study villages in Rajasthan. These variables include farm and non-farm production, employment, livelihoods, and the socio-economic characteristics of different classes in the villages. We further studied, from a class perspective, issues of household asset ownership and indebtedness, and access to the basic amenities of modern life. The village studies presented analyses of sectional deprivation, particularly with respect to caste hierarchies and oppression. Taken together, the analysis of the two villages, based on data from census surveys, attempts to provide a distinct perspective on the rural economy of the State.

Bibliography

Bakshi, Aparajita (2008), "Social Inequality in Land Ownership in India: A Study with Particular Reference to West Bengal", *Social Scientist*, 36 (9–10).

Bakshi, Aparajita (2015), "Nature of Income Diversification in Village India with a Special Focus on Dalit Households", Project Report submitted to Indian Council for Social Science Research, Foundation for Agrarian Studies, Bangalore.

Bandyopadhyay, D. (1986), "Land Reforms in India: An Analysis", *Economic and Political Weekly*, 21 (25–26), 21–28 June.

Census of India (2013), *Census of India, 2011: Primary Census Abstract, Data Highlights, India, Series I*, Office of the Registrar General and Census Commissioner, India.

Chavan, Pallavi (2005), "Banking Sector Reforms and Growth and Distribution of Rural Banking in India", in V.K. Ramachandran and Madhura Swaminathan (eds), *Financial Liberalisation and Rural Credit*, Tulika Books, New Delhi.

Chavan, Pallavi (2012), "Debt of Rural Households in India: A Note on the All-India Debt and Investment Survey", *Review of Agrarian Studies*, 2 (1), January–June.

Chavan, Pallavi (2013), "Public Banks and Financial Intermediation in India: The Phases of Nationalisation, Liberalisation and Inclusion", unpublished.

Communist Party of India (Marxist) (CPI[M]) (2009), "For the Universal Right to Food Security"; url: http://cpim.org/node/1379.

Dhar, Niladri Sekhar (2013a), "On Days of Employment of Rural Labour Households", *Review of Agrarian Studies*, 2 (2), July–December; url: http://www.ras.org.in/on_days_of_employment_of_rural_labour_households.

Dhar, Niladri Sekhar, with Kaur, Navpreet (2013b), 'Features of Rural Underemployment in India: Evidence from Nine Villages', *Review of Agrarian Studies*, 3 (1), January–June.

Ellis, Frank (2000), *Rural Livelihoods and Diversity in Developing Countries*, Oxford University Press, Oxford.

Farrington, John, Deshingkar, Priya, Johnson, Craig, and Start, Daniel (eds) (2006), *Policy Windows and Livelihood Futures: Prospects of Poverty Reduction in Rural India*, Oxford University Press, New Delhi.

Foundation for Agrarian Studies (FAS) (2012), "Child Well-being, Schooling and Living

Standards: Report on Three Villages of Rajasthan", Foundation for Agrarian Studies, July; url: http://www.agrarianstudies.org/UserFiles/File/Rajasthan_Report.pdf.

Foundation for Agrarian Studies (FAS) (2015), "Manual on Income Calculation and Questionnaire", unpublished.

Ghasiram (2007), *Kisan andolan janit chetana aur swadhinata sangram: Rajasthan ke sandarbh mein (The freedom struggle and the consciousness generated by the peasant movement: in the context of Rajasthan)*, Aalekh Publications, Jaipur.

Government of India (GoI) (1966), *Implementation of Land Reforms: A Review by the Land Reforms Implementation Committee of the National Development Council*, Planning Commission, Government of India, New Delhi.

Government of India (GoI) (1990), *Rural Labour Enquiry – Report on Indebtedness among Rural Labour Households – 1983*, Ministry of Labour and Employment, New Delhi.

Government of India (GoI) (1991), *Final Population Totals – Series 1*, New Delhi.

Government of India (GoI) (2001), *Provisional Population Totals: Rural and Urban Distribution for India and States/Union Territories*, New Delhi.

Government of India (GoI) (2004), *Rural Labour Enquiry – Report on Indebtedness among Rural Labour Households – 1999–2000*, Ministry of Labour and Employment, New Delhi.

Government of India (GoI) (2008), *Annual Report: 2007–08*, Ministry of Rural Development, Government of India, New Delhi.

Government of India (GoI) (2009), *Annual Report 2008–09*, Ministry of Human Resource Development; url: http://mhrd.gov.in/sites/upload_files/mhrd/files/document-reports/AR2008-09.pdf

Government of India (GoI) (2010), *Rural Labour Enquiry – Report on Indebtedness among Rural Labour Households – 2004–05*, Ministry of Labour and Employment, New Delhi.

Government of Rajasthan (2008), *Rajasthan Human Development Report (An Update – 2008)*; url: http://statistics.rajasthan.gov.in/Details/hd_final.pdf

Government of Tripura (2007), *Human Development Report 2007*, Government of Tripura, Agartala; url: http://tripura.nic.in/hdr/welcome.html.

Iyer, Gopal K. (1995a), "Agrarian Transition in Rajasthan: Role of Tenancy Reforms", in B.N. Yugandhar and P.S. Datta (eds), *Land Reforms in India*, Volume 2: *Rajasthan: Feudalism and Change*, Sage Publications, New Delhi.

Iyer, Gopal K. (1995b), "Implementation of Land Ceiling Programme in Rajasthan", in B.N. Yugandhar and P.S. Datta (eds), *Land Reforms in India*, Volume 2: *Rajasthan: Feudalism and Change*, Sage Publications, New Delhi.

Jatav, Manoj, and Sen, Sucharita (2013), "Drivers of non-farm employment in rural India", *Economic and Political Weekly*, 48 (26–27), June.

Naithani, Shobhita (2009), "Caught in a sorrowful yarn", *Tehelka*, 6 (38), 26 September.

National Sample Survey Organisation (NSSO) (1998), "Note on Household Assets and Liabilities as on 30.06.91: NSS 48[h] Round (Jan–Dec 1992)", *Sarvekshana*, 22 (2), October–December.

National Sample Survey Organisation (NSSO) (2005), *Household Indebtedness in India as on 30–06–2002, Report No. 501*, New Delhi.

Pande, Ram (1974), *Agrarian Movement in Rajasthan*, University Publishers, Delhi.

Pande, Ram (1982), *People's Movement in Rajasthan (Selection from Originals)*, Vol. 1, Shodhak, Jaipur.

Pande, Ram (1986), *People's Movement in Rajasthan (Selection from Originals)*, Vol. 2: *Bijay Singh Pathik Papers*, Shodhak, Jaipur.

Ram, Pema (1986), *Agrarian Movement in Rajasthan: 1913–1947 AD*, Panchsheel Prakashan, Jaipur.

Ramachandran, V.K. (2010), "Dungariya Village, Southern Rajasthan", *Critical Asian Studies*, 42 (2), June.

Ramachandran, V.K. (2011), "The State of Agrarian Relations in India Today", *The Marxist*, 27 (1–2): 52–89, January–June.

Ramachandran, V.K., and Rawal, Vikas (2010), "The Impact of Liberalization and Globalization on India's Agrarian Economy", *Global Labour Journal*, 1 (1): 56–91; url: http://digitalcommons.mcmaster.ca/globallabour/vol1/iss1/5.

Ramachandran, V.K., Rawal, Vikas, and Swaminathan, Madhura (2010), *Socio-Economic Surveys of Three Villages in Andhra Pradesh: A Study of Agrarian Relations*, Tulika Books, New Delhi.

Ramachandran, V.K., and Swaminathan, Madhura (2005), "Introduction", in V.K. Ramachandran and Madhura Swaminathan (eds.), *Financial Liberalisation and Rural Credit*, Tulika Books, New Delhi.

Ramachandran, V.K., Swaminathan, Madhura, and Rawal, Vikas (2002), "How have hired workers fared? A case study of women workers from an Indian village, 1977 to 1999", *The Indian Journal of Labour Economics*, 45 (2), April–June.

Ramakumar, R., and Chavan, Pallavi (2011), "Changes in the Number of Rural Bank Branches in India, 1991 to 2008", *Review of Agrarian Studies*, 1 (1), January–June.

Rawal, Vikas (2006), "The Labour Process in Rural Haryana India: A Field Report from Two Villages", *Journal of Agrarian Change*, 6 (4), October.

Rawal, Vikas (2008), "Estimation of Rural Household Incomes in India: Selected Methodological Issues", paper presented at "Studying Village Economies in India: A Colloquium on Methodology", Chalsa; url: http://www.fas.org.in/UserFiles/File/S5_Rawal_Estimation_of_Rural_Household_Incomes_in_India.pdf

Rawal, Vikas (2011), "Statistics on Elementary School Education in Rural India", *Review of Agrarian Studies*, 1 (2): 179–201, July–December; url: http://ras.org.in/statistics_on_elementary_school_education_in_rural_india.

Rawal, Vikas (2013a), "Cost of cultivation and farm business incomes in India", CEI Working Paper Series 2012–15, Center for Economic Institutions, Institute of Economic Research, Hitotsubashi University, March; url: http://hermes-ir.lib.hitu.ac.jp/rs/bitstream/10086/25635/1/wp2012-15.pdf

Rawal, Vikas (2013b), "Socio-Economic Surveys of Selected Villages in Rajasthan: A Report Prepared for the University Grants Commission", unpublished.

Rawal, Vikas, and Swaminathan, Madhura (2011), "Returns from Crop Cultivation and Scale of Production", paper presented at the workshop on "Policy Options and Investment Priorities for Accelerating Agricultural Productivity and Development in India", New Delhi, 8–9 November; url: http://www.igidr.ac.in/newspdf/srijit/PP-069-21b

Reserve Bank of India (RBI) (2008), *Report on Currency and Finance: 2006–08*, Mumbai.

Reserve Bank of India (RBI), *Banking Statistics/Basic Statistical Returns of Scheduled Commercial Banks in India*, Mumbai, various issues.

Rudolph, Susanne Hoeber, and Rudolph, Lloyd L. (2011), "From Landed Class to Middle Class: Rajput Adaptation in Rajasthan", in Amita Baviskar and Raka Ray (eds), *Elite and Everyman: The Cultural Politics of the Indian Middle Classes*, Routledge, New Delhi.

Sarkar, Anupam (2014), "Mechanisation in Contemporary Indian Agriculture", Ph.D. thesis, University of Calcutta, unpublished.

Saxena, H.C. (1952), "Abolition of Jagirdari: A Landmark in the History of Rajasthan", *Economic and Political Weekly*, 16 February.

Sen, Abhijit, and Bhatia, M.S. (2004), *Cost of Cultivation and Farm Income*, Volume 14 of *State of the Indian Farmer: A Millennium Study*, Academic Foundation in association with Department of Agriculture and Cooperation, Ministry of Agriculture, Government of India, New Delhi.

Sharma, Brij Kishor (1990), *Peasant Movements in Rajasthan*, Pointer Publishers, Jaipur.

Sharma, Brij Kishor (1992), *Samantwad Evam Kisan Sangharsh (Feudalism and Peasant Struggle)*, Pointer Publishers, Jaipur.

Shetty, S.L. (2005), "Regional, Sectoral and Functional Distribution of Bank Credit", in V.K. Ramachandran and Madhura Swaminathan (eds), *Financial Liberalisation and Rural Credit*, Tulika Books, New Delhi.

Singh, Akhilesh Kumar, and Singh, Rao Jaswant (2009), "Life's Cheap in the Cotton Fields of Gujarat", *The Times of India*, 28 August.

Singhvi, B.L. (2004), *"Mewar ka adivasi vidroh: Angrezi samrajya aur samantwadi gathjod ke khilaf Rajasthan ke swatantrata senani Motilalji Tejawat ka bahaduripoorn sangharsh aur sabak, vartaman mein chunautiyan aur hamare kartavya"* ("The adivasi revolt of Mewar: The courageous struggle of Motilalji Tejawat, freedom fighter of Rajasthan, against the alliance of British imperialism and feudalism, and lessons from the struggle, future challenges and our duties")*,* Udaipur, unpublished.

Sisson, Richard J. (1966), "Institutionalisation and Style in Rajasthan Politics", *Asian Survey*, 6 (11), November.

Sisson, Richard J. (1969), "Peasant Movements and Political Mobilisation: The Jats of Rajasthan", *Asian Survey*, 9 (12), December.

Sisson, Richard J. (1971), *The Congress Party in Rajasthan: Political Integration and Institution Building in an Indian State,* University of California Press, Berkeley and Los Angeles.

Srinivas, V. (1995), "Tenancy Reforms in Nagaur District", in B.N. Yugandhar and P.S. Datta (eds), *Land Reforms in India*, Volume 2: *Rajasthan: Feudalism and Change*, Sage Publications, New Delhi.

Stern, Robert W. (1988), "The Cat and the Lion: Jaipur State in the British Raj", in *Monographs and Theoretical Studies in Sociology and Anthropology in Honour of Nels Anderson*, No. 21, E.J. Brill, Leiden.

Surjit, V. (2008), *Farm Business Incomes*, Ph.D. thesis, University of Calcutta, unpublished.

Swaminathan, Madhura (1991), "Segmentation, Collateral Undervaluation, and the Rate of Interest in Agrarian Credit", *Cambridge Journal of Economics*, 15 (2).

Swaminathan, Madhura (2012), "Who has Access to Formal Credit in Rural India? Evidence from Four Villages", *Review of Agrarian Studies*, 2 (1), January–June.

Swaminathan, Madhura, and Rawal, Vikas (2011), "Is India Really a Country of Low Income Inequality? Observations from Eight Villages", *Review of Agrarian Studies*, 1 (1), January–June; url: http://ras.org.in/is_india_really_a_country_of_low_income_inequality_observations from eight_villages.

Thomas, Jayan Jose, and Das, Yasodhara (2014), "A Note on Migration from Rural India: Evidence from PARI Villages", paper presented at the Tenth Anniversary Conference of the Foundation for Agrarian Studies, Kochi, 9–12 January.

Tod, James (1920), *Annals and Antiquities of Rajasthan or the Central and Western Rajput States of India*, edited with an Introduction and Notes by William Crooke, Volume III, Oxford University Press, Humphrey.

United Nations Development Programme (UNDP) (2002), *Rajasthan Human Development Report 2002*; url: http://www.in.undp.org/content/dam/india/docs/human_development_report_rajasthan_2002_full_report.pdf

Yugandhar, B.N., and Datta, P.S. (eds) (1995), *Land Reforms in India*, Volume 2: *Rajasthan: Feudalism and Change*, Sage Publications, New Delhi.

Presentations made at the "Meeting on the Results from Village Surveys, Rajasthan Round, Project on Agrarian Relations (PARI)", Jaipur, 3–5 March 2012

Athreya, Venkatesh with Dutta, Koustav, "Population, schooling and education".

Bakshi, Aparajita, "Household incomes".

Dhar, Niladri, and Kaur, Navpreet, "Wage rates".

Dhar, Niladri, and Kaur, Navpreet with Adhikari, Nabanita, "Employment".

Ramachandran, V.K., "Migration, non-farm employment in Rewasi".

Ramachandran, V.K., "Report on the survey of Dungariya village".

Ramachandran, V.K. with Kaur, Navpreet, "Socio-economic classes in survey villages".

Rawal, Vikas, "Agricultural mechanisation in 25 F Gulabewala".

Rawal, Vikas, and Kaur, Navpreet with Adhikari, Nabanita, "Labour absorption in agriculture".

Rawal, Vikas with Sarkar, Biplab, "Land, tenancy and irrigation; crop pattern, and yields and farm business incomes".

Rawal, Vikas with Sarkar, Biplab, Bhaduri, Sumit, and Das, Arindam, "Land, tenancy and irrigation; crop pattern, and yields and farm business incomes".

Singh, Shamsher, "Household amenities".
Swaminathan, Madhura, "Income inequality in 25 F Gulabewala".
Swaminathan, Madhura with Dutta, Koustav, "Household asset holdings".
Swaminathan, Madhura with Roy, Shantanu De, "Household indebtedness".
Usami, Y., and Ramakumar, R., "Report on NREGA in Rajasthan".